I0567402

Persian

Empire

The Conflicts Between the Achaemenid Empire and the Greek City-states

(Starting From the Achaemenid Empire Through the Parthian Sasanian)

Essie Neill

Published By **Tyson Maxwell**

Essie Neill

Persian Empire: The Conflicts Between the Achaemenid Empire and the Greek City-states (Starting From the Achaemenid Empire Through the Parthian Sasanian)

ISBN   978-1-998769-62-9

No part of this guidebook shall be reproduced in any form without permission in writing from the publisher except in the case of brief quotations embodied in critical articles or reviews.

Legal & Disclaimer

The information contained in this ebook is not designed to replace or take the place of any form of medicine or professional medical advice. The information in this ebook has been provided for educational & entertainment purposes only.

The information contained in this book has been compiled from sources deemed reliable, and it is accurate to the best of the Author's knowledge; however, the Author cannot guarantee its accuracy and validity and cannot be held liable for any errors or omissions. Changes are periodically made to this book. You must consult your doctor or get professional medical advice before using any of the suggested remedies, techniques, or information in this book.

Upon using the information contained in this book, you agree to hold harmless the Author from and against any damages, costs, and expenses, including any legal fees potentially resulting from the application of any of the information provided by this guide. This disclaimer applies to any damages or injury caused by the use and application, whether directly or indirectly, of any advice or information presented, whether for breach of contract, tort, negligence, personal injury, criminal intent, or under any other cause of action.

You agree to accept all risks of using the information presented inside this book. You need to consult a professional medical practitioner in order to ensure you are both able and healthy enough to participate in this program.

Table of contents

Chapter 1: Name and Area...................... 1

Chapter 2: The Early History of the Empire
.... 4

Chapter 3: The Wars with Greece 16

Chapter 4: The 2nd Egyptian Conquest.. 33

Chapter 5: Why the Empire Fails............ 39

Chapter 6: Cultural Factors In Society 45

Chapter 1: Name and Area

The Persian Empire is a great empire that was a long time ago.

The Persian Empire's most common territory was the present-day Iran. The Persians had a profound influence on all surrounding countries. Their style, music, rule and culture had an impact on science and the formation nations.

The Achaemenid Empire is renowned for its effectiveness in enforcing a centralized, government administration using satraps. Because of its success, other empires adopted similar systems.

You can find out more in this book on the history of this empire.

The First Persian Empire had another name, the Achaemenid Empire.

It was an ancient Iranian empire that was based in Western Asia. The capital was established by Cyrus I in 550 BC. It reached its peak in the time of Xerxes 1, who dominated many older areas of Greece.

The Achaemenid empire's largest area of territory ran from the Balkans in the west and Eastern Europe in east to the Indus River in the East. The empire's total area was 5.5 million kilometers. It also covered more territory than any other historical empire (2.1,000,000 square miles).

The Persians established the empire in the Persian Plateau, south.

Cyrus rose to power from this region and defeated both the Average Empire--ofwhich he had been king--and Lydia, the Neo-Babylonian Empire. Developing the Achaemenid Empire in the process.

Alexander the Great (an impassioned admirer Cyrus's Great) ruled many Achaemenid Kingdoms by 330 BC.

Alexander's demise saw the Ptolemaic King and the Seleucid Imperial take control of much of the empire's previous terrain. The Parthian Empire was able to regain control over the plateau's Iranian elites by the second Century BC.

The Parsa were the first nomadic people to establish the empire. Their continually moving world was known as Parsua. Persis was their main focus around 850 BC.

"Persia," the name of "Persia", is a combination Greek and Latin words.

Chapter 2: The Early History of the Empire

Nomadic Persians founded the Achaemenid Kingdom. The Persians are an Iranian people that first arrived in Iran about 1,000 BC. They also lived with the native Elamites throughout an area that encompassed northwestern Iran, the Zagros Mountains and Persis.

The Neo-Assyrian Empire (912--609 BC) was their ruler for hundreds of years. It concentrated in northern Mesopotamia. The Persians lived in the western Iranian Plateau as nomadic pastoralists. Another Iranian tribe, the Medes (a group of Iranian tribes), established a temporary empire. They played a pivotal role in the conquering the Assyrians. Therefore, the Achaemenid State is not the first Iranian empire.

Anshan, a Elamite city near Marvdasht, was originally ruled by the Achaemenids.

Their title "Kingshan" was a derivative Elamite title called "Kingsa and Anshan".

The identity of the first Kings in Anshan is under dispute. The Cyrus Cylinder (the oldest Achaemenid extant genealogy) states that the Anshan Kings were Teispes II, Cyrus I and Cambyses I. Also known as Cyrus II, who established the empire. (The later Behistun Engraving by Darius the Great claims that Teispes is the child of Achaemenes. Darius is also said to have come down from Teispes though no other texts mention Achaemenes. According to Herodotus' Histories Cyrus, the Great, was the child Cambyses I of Mandane of Media.

Cyrus revolted in 553 BC against Typical Empire. In 550 BC he defeated the Medes, taking Astyages & catching Ecbatana.

Cyrus took control over Ecbatana and declared himself Astyages' successor. This gave him presumed command over the entire empire. Astyages' empire was acquired by him. He also dealt with the Medes' territorial dispute with Lydia and the Neo-Babylonian Emperor.

King Croesus from Lydia wanted to profit from the new global situation by expanding into Mean territory in Asia Minor.

Cyrus led a counteroffensive that defeated Croesus' soldiers and also led to Sardis' capture and the fall of the Lydian kingdom in 546 BC. Cyrus left Pactyes as the person responsible for gathering tribute in Lydia. Pactyes, however, staged a revolt against Cyrus shortly after Cyrus had fled.

Cyrus took Pactyes. He dispatched Mazares, the Typical general, to put an end to the insurrection. Harpagus took steps to lower the ranks of all the cities involved in the rebellion after Mazares was killed. Lydia was ruled by Harpagus for 4 years.

Many tributaries to the Mean Empire rebelled against Cyrus believing that their situation had changed after Ecbatana was lost by the Medes to the Persians.

Cyrus was thus required to wage war against Bactria (and the nomadic Saka) in Central Asia. At the time these projects were underway, Cyrus set up various fort towns throughout Central Asia.

Although little is known about Persian and Babylonian relations between 547 BC & 539 BC, it seems very likely that both empires shared some years before the 540--539 BC conflict and Babylon's fall.

Cyrus defeated the Babylonians by Opis in October 539 BC. After dominating Sippar without fighting, Cyrus took Babylon on October 12th.

Cyrus used propaganda as a way to portray himself and the remarkable order that had been destroyed by Nabonidus.

Cyrus is also known in Hebrew Bible as Yahweh's greasy for his actions in defeating Babylon. He is the one who released Judah's banished persons and allowed the rehabilitation of the majority Jerusalem, which includes the 2nd Temple.

Cyrus is believed that he died in Central Asia on a military expedition against the Massagetae in 553 BC. Cambyses II, his older child, became his successor. Bardiya however was given a significant area in Central Asia.

Cambyses, a conqueror of Phoenicia/Cyprus in 525 BC, was already planning to attack Egypt with the Persian Navy he had just created.

Psamtik II, the son of the popular Pharaoh Amasis III, was made a successor by him in

526 BC. It led to the loss to the Persians of important Egyptian allies. Psamtik sent his army to the Nile Delta at Pelusium.

He was severely squashed by Persians at the Battle of Pelusium before fleeing to Memphis, where he escaped to be beat and held by the Persians.

Herodotus shows Cambyses as openly hostile toward the Egyptian people, gods, cults and temples. His focus is on the assassination attempt on the spiritual bull Apis.

He claims that these events made him insane and led to his murder of his brother Bardiya. Herodotus asserts that he was secretly killed.

Cambyses has gone mad, and he concludes that all classical writers have echoed the themes of Cambyses' impiety and madness. This assumption is false, however, because the Apis epitaph (524

BC) states that Cambyses took part in Apis' funeral events, while impersonating a pharaoh.

Cambyses' victory over Egypt saw the Libyans and Greeks in Cyrene and Barca (modern-day Eastern Libya) give up and remember him without any battle.

Cambyses also developed attack plans for Carthage, Ammon's sanctuary, and Ethiopia. Herodotus states that the marine intrusion on Carthage by the Phoenicians was cancelled. Although history experts dispute the claim, it was cancelled.

Cambyses, by contrast, focused his efforts on the Empire's other 2 wars. These were meant to consolidate the Empire's tactical position on Africa by recording and developing the Kingdom of Mero.

To this end, he constructed a fort in Elephantine, primarily made up of Jewish soldiers, and stayed there during

Cambyses' rule. Both Ammon's intruders and Ethiopia's were unsuccessful.

Herodotus said that the intrusion of Ethiopia failed because of Cambyses' insanity. He also didn't have enough supplies for his men. But historical evidence suggests that the exploration was not a failure. The citadel at the 2nd Cataract of the Nile bordering Egypt and Kush remained functional during the Achaemenid Period.

Many different opinions exist about the events after Cambyses' passing and Bardiya's reign.

Herodotus states that even though Bardiya's assassination was done in complete secrecy most Persians believed that he was still alive. Due to their physical similarities (Smerdis in Herodotus' accounts), 2 Magi had the power to rise up against Cambyses. The throne was also able for one Magi to imitate Bardiya. Ctesias states that Cambyses killed Bardiya and immediately made Sphendadates his satrap of Bactria due to a striking physical similarity. Cambyses' confidants then planned to depose him, and Sphendadates was made king under the pretense that Bardiya.

According to the Behistun Engraving by Darius, the Great, Gaumata was a magus who impersonated Bardiya. Cambyses discovered more about the causes of the revolt during the summer season in 522 BC, and they set off to return from Egypt.

Bardiya was nevertheless injured in Syria, and he died from gangrene.

Darius' story may be the first. However, while prosperous chroniclers focus on the essential facts of the story, specifically that Bardiya was impersonated as a magus, it is possible Darius concocted the story to cover his own usurpation.

Pierre Briant, Iranologist says that Bardiya's legal claim to the throne was not quashed by Cambyses. He waited to die in the summer season 522 BC.

Briant claims that Darius' deceitfulness has been accepted by most people today. However, Briant also asserts that nothing is known with certainty right now, given all available evidence.

According to the Behistun Engraving Gaumata ruled over 7 months before being deposed by Darius the Great (Darius I), in 522 BC. Despite being penalized the Magi continued and, one year after Gaumata (the first pseudo-Smerdis) died, Vahyazdta (the second pseudo-Smerdis) attempted a coup. Despite the coup's initial success, it failed.

Herodotus said that the regional management challenged the ideal type of federal government to govern the empire.

Macedonians and Persians were strangers until Amyntas the Macedonian Queen abandoned her world in order to make way for the Persians. This was around 512-511. Macedonia was overthrown by Darius the Great (521 - 486) in 513 when a large Achaemenid army attacked Balkans, and attempted to conquer the European Scythians living to the north of Danube.

Darius' army ruled several Thracian villages and nearly all areas that touch the European side of the Black Sea. Bubares, a Persian ruler, married Amyntas' daughter Gygaea. There were tons of Persian nobility and Macedonian nobility who intermarried.

Due to their connections with Bubares families, the Macedonian emperors

Amyntassas as well as Alexander maintained strong relations with Persian kings Darius (and Xerxes) the Great. Persia and Macedonia had common interests in the Balkans. Persia helped Macedonia rise indirectly to power. However, Macedonia could get a lot with Persian aid at the expense of some Balkan tribes such as the Paeonians and Greeks.

Generally, the Macedonians were "prepared to benefit Persian allies," with Macedonian combatants fighting in Xerxes' army against Athens.

Macedonians were described by the Persians both as Yauna (" Ionians") and as Yauna ("Yauna" for Greeks.

Chapter 3: The Wars with Greece

The Ionian Revolt of 499 BC and other revolts in Aeolis. Doris, Cyprus, Caria and Caria were part of a series that was designed to rebel against Persian control over Asia Minor. It lasted between 499 and 493 BC.

The revolt was inspired by the protests of the Greek cities in Asia Minor against the Persia sent out autocrats to them. Also, the deeds 2 Milesian autocrats Histiaeus & Aristagoras. Aristagoras (then-tyrant of Miletus) organized a joint exploration along with the Persian satrap Artaphernes in order to take Naxos 499 BC. Aristagoras, fearful of being deposed as totalitarian made the mistake of abandoning the operation and urging all of Ionia, including Darius the Great, to revolt against him.

The Persians then continued to ruin the cities along west coast which withstood them. In the end, they enforced a peace settlement at Ionia in 493 BC that was generally regarded as just-and-fair.

The Ionian Revolt marked the start of the Greco-Persian Wars. It was the first major conflict between Greece and its Achaemenid empire. Darius promised to punish Athens and Eretria if they supported the revolt by bringing Asia Minor again into the Persian fold.

In addition, knowing that the political situation in Greece presented a continuous risk to his Empire's stability he chose to control all of Greece. The invasion's initial objective was to reintegrate Balkan Peninsula's possessions into the empire. After the Ionian Revolt, Persian control had decreased over these territories.

Mardonius, a Persian general, subjugated Thrace in 492 BC. He made Macedon a fully subordinate section of the empire.

Macedon had been a vassal of the empire since the late sixth-century BC but retained a lot of autonomy. After the Battle at Marathon, 490 BC, the Persian armies fell to the Athenians, and Darius died prior to launching an invasion in Greece.

The child of Darius, Xerxes (455-8465 BC, Old Persian Xayra "Hero Amongst Kings") was promised that he would complete the task. He planned to lead a massive attack against Greece. His army marched through Greece from the north in spring 480 BC. He encountered little or no resistance in Macedonia/Thessaly, but was held back for 3 days at Thermopylae, by a small Greek force. Both sides suffered from huge storms, which made a coordinated marine battle at Artemisium strategically indecisive.

The fight at Thermopylae was called off by the Greeks after they found out their defeat. The Persians won, and they gained undisputed power over Artemisium as well as the Aegean.

After his success at Thermopylae Xerxes demolished the left Athens, and prepared for battle with the Greeks on the Isthmus of Corinth. At the Battle of Salamis (480 BC), the Greeks defeated a Persian fleet and pushed Xerxes towards Sardis.

Mardonius's Greek land army under Mardonius retook Athens in 479 BC. The Persians' loss at Mycale proved to be a decisive defeat. Athens was overthrown by the Greek cities, who revolted.

Artaxerxes III, his oldest child, took the place of Xerxes. Elamite was no longer the preferred main language. Aramaic grew in popularity at the time of his rule. The solar calendar was adopted by the country as its calendar throughout this age. Artaxerxes

III made Zoroastrianism the official state religion.

Persia won the Battle of Eurymedon (469-466 BC) and ended military engagement between Greece & Persia. Artaxerxes, I was elected to power and implemented a new Persian strategy of funding the Greek competitors.

Because of this, Athenians were pressured to move Delian League's treasurer from Delos towards the Athenian Acropolis. This monetary strategy caused more bloodshed when the Greeks invaded Cyprus at the Battle of Cyprus in 449 BC. Athens, Argos and Persia checked the Peace of Callias in 449 BC, after Cimon failed throughout this objective.

Artaxerxes   Artaxerxes   Following Themistocles' victory at Battle of Salamis, I expelled him from Athens and granted him asylum.

Artaxerxes' death in Susa, 424 BC, saw his body given to the Naqsh-e Rustam Necropolis. It was there that he had a former burial ground. Persia was accustomed to queens building their own tombs as soon as they were alive. Xerxes III, Artaxerxes 1's oldest, and only lawful, child, was immediately made his successor.

Pharnacyas & Menostanes intoxicated him, killing him on the orders and instructions of his invalid brother Sogdianus. He had seemingly received the obligation to his territories after only a few short days on his throne.

Ochus was his half-brother and ruled him for six months. He then abducted him. Ochus had pledged that he would not die from hunger, toxin, or the sword. Sogdianus was made to suffocate in ash. Ochus received the title King Darius I after this. Darius's power to protect his reign was enough to fill the power vacuum.

At Tissaphernes' insistence, Darius II supported Athens before Sparta. However in 407 BC, Cyrus the Younger (Darius' child) was selected to help Tissaphernes. Sparta was then given all the support it required to defeat Athens.

Darius became unwell and passed away in Babylon the same year. Amyrtaeus (an Egyptian rebel) had the chance to challenge Persian sovereignty over Egypt by his death. Parysatis, Darius' Babylonian spouse, asked him to crown her 2nd youngest child Cyrus (the Yerner) on his final day. Queen Parysatis chose Cyrus to be her oldest child Artaxerxes.

The Tissaphernes who had been expelled came to the crowning day of the new king in order to warn him that Cyrus, his younger brother (the Younger), was planning on killing him at the time the routine took place. Artaxerxes could have sent Cyrus to prison, and had their mom Parysatis not intervened.

Cyrus was then sent back to Lydia as Satrap. There he organized an armed rebellion. Cyrus amassed a huge army, which included 10000 Greek mercenaries. Then he advanced into Persia.

Artaxerxes II of the regal Persian army defeated Cyrus' army at Cunaxa in 413 BC. Cyrus was also killed. The 10 thousand Greek Mercenaries, which included Xenophon and were deep in Persian territory, were at risk of being attacked.

They attempted to find others to fill their skills, but eventually had to return to Greece.

Artaxerxes III ruled the longest Achaemenid monarchs. Numerous monoliths from the period were built during this 45 year period of relative peace, stability and stability. Artaxerxes established Persepolis again as the capital. He greatly expanded it.

Ecbatana's summer capital, Ecbatana, was also beautifully enlarged with gilded posts and silver- and copper roofing tiles.

His rule is also associated with Zoroastrian religion's extraordinary growth. Zoroastrianism spread from Armenia through Asia Minor to the Levant during this period. The purpose of temple building and construction was spiritual, but it was not completely selfless, since it provided a substantial source for cash.

The Babylonian Queens' principle of a forcible temple tax had been adopted by the Achaemenids. All locals were required to pay a one-tenth tithe to the temple closest their land, or to another source of income. Nabonidus came up with an innovative idea called the Quppu Sha Sha Sha (or "king's pocket") that allowed the ruler to receive a share of this wealth. Artaxerxes has a reputation for being a pleasant man who lacked the moral stability and ability to rule in retrospection. 6 centuries later Ardeshir I would see himself as Artaxerxes' son, a testament to Artaxerxes' Midpoint in Persian thought.

Artaxerxes III ended up getting involved in a dispute between Persia and its previous allies, The Spartans. These Spartans attacked Asia Minor under Agesilaus I. Artaxerxes III sponsored the Spartans' challengers, including the Athenians. Thebans. and Corinthians to divert their focus away from Greek issues.

These aids were able to enable the Spartans take part in Corinthian War. Artaxerxes II renounced his allies, and negotiated with Sparta 387 BC. This allowed his former allies the Treaty of Antalcidas to reach an agreement. The treaty gave Persians control of Aeolis and Ionia, both Greek cities on the Anatolian Coast, while Sparta gained control of Greece's mainland.

He led a project against Cadusians in 385 BC. Artaxerxes III had more trouble with Egypt II, who had rebelled against him at the beginning of his reign despite his success over the Greeks.

While there was no genuine effort to conquer Egypt in 373 BC it was stopped by the Persians who managed to drive out an Egyptian--Simple venture to take over Phoenicia his final years. He put down the Satraps' Revolt, 362 BC to 372. It is believed that he married several women. Stateira was his main courtesan, until she was poisoned at the hands of Artaxerxes I's mom Parysatis in around 400 BC.

Aspasia was a Phocaean Greek women. She was also his main marriage partner.

Artaxerxes II died 358 BC. Artaxerxes his son Artaxerxes II succeeded him. Artaxerxes, the Third forced Athens in 358 BC to sign a peace accord that required Athens' armies from Asia Minor to surrender to their enemies and recognize their independence. Artaxerxes launched the offensive against insurgent Cadusians, but the emperors of both armies were pacified by him. Darius Codomannus, who rose to the Persian crown as Darius III was just one of the many successful people to emerge from this conflict.

Artaxerxes Third ordered that all Asia Minor's soldiers be disintegrated, believing that they could not provide peace in the west and these fighters had given the western satraps the resources to revolt.

Artabazos of Phrygia II of Phrygia was the opposite and disobeyed orders and sought Athens' support in a rebellion against the king. Athens offered support to Sardis. Orontes, a Mysia woman, helped Artabazos defeat Artaxerxes III's army in 354 BC.

They were defeated by Artaxerxes III III's army in 353 BC. The alliance was then dissolved. Orontes was forgiven by the Emperor, but Artabazos fled to protect Philip II at Macedon's Court. Artaxerxes initiated a project in 351 BC that was to recover Egypt which had rebelled under Artaxerxes II. Thebes helped to stop an insurgency in Asia Minor. Artaxerxes enlisted Nectanebo II and marched into Egypt with an army.

Nectanebo, with the help of mercenaries led the by the Greek generals Diophantus & Lamius, caused a crushing defeat upon the Persians after one year of fighting to overthrow the Egyptian Pharaoh. Artaxerxes was forced from Egypt to leave, and his plans to retake Egypt were delayed. Not long after the loss, disobediences began to emerge in Phoenicia as well Asia Minor and Cyprus.

Artaxerxes gave the victory over the Cyprian insurgents at Caria to Idrieus, prince from Caria, in 343 BC. He used 8,000 Greeks mercenaries and 40 triremes ordered by Phocion and Evagoras.

Idrieus had success in reducing Cyprus. Artaxerxes launched another offensive against Sidon. They ordered Mazaeus the Cilician slave and Belesys the Syrian satrap to get into the city.

Tennes, Sidonese's emperor, was supported in his victory by 40,000 Greeks mercenaries. He was sent out by Nectanebo 2 and ordered Coach of

Rhodes. As a consequence, the Persian fighters were forced out of Phoenicia.

Artaxerxes commanded a 330,000-man army against Sidon. Artaxerxes had 300,000 feet men, 30,000 troops, three-hundred triremes, five-hundred transportations and arrangement ships.

After assembling his force, he turned to the Greeks for help.

Despite Sparta's and Athens' rejections of his request to help them, he was able employ 1,000 Theban heavy arm hoplites (under Lacrates), 3 thousand Argives (under Nicostratus) and 6 000 olians/Ionians and Dorians.

Although it was small in numbers, not more than ten thousands men, the Greek support provided the foundation of his force. The Egyptian Greek mercenaries joined him later, and were mostly responsible for the success of the exploration.

Tennes' willpower had been so weakened by Artaxerxes' method that he tried for his own pardon. He gave Sidon's most vital occupants over to the Persian king, and then confessed Artaxerxes within town defenses.

Artaxerxes sent the 100 residents into prison with javelins. Artaxerxes then sentenced the remaining supplicants to the exact opposite fate when more than five-hundred came out to beg his mercy. Artaxerxes (or the Sidon locals) set fire to the city.

The blaze claimed the life of 40,000 people.

Artaxerxes made a huge profit selling the remains to speculators, who wanted to recover their financial investment. Tennes was then executed by Artaxerxes.

Artaxerxes later killed the Jews who had backed Hyrcania's invasion on the Caspian Sea's South Coast.

Chapter 4: The 2nd Egyptian Conquest

The fall of Sidon was followed by the intrusion into Egypt. Artaxerxes was supported by 14,000 Greeks in Asia Minor. He divided the men into three groups, with each having a Persian or a Greek as the helm. Coach of Rhodes (Lactrates), Nicostratus from Argos (Nicostratus of Argos) and Coach of Thebes (Coach of Rhodes) were the Greek leaders. Rhossaces Aristazanes, Bagoas, and Bagoas, who was the chief eunuch, led the Persians. Nectanebo III fought back with a 100,000-strong army. This included 20,000 Greeks mercenaries. Nectanebo III occupied the Nile, its various branches, and with his naval skills.

Nectanebo, II, could have been expected that he would mount a sustained, if not triumphant resistance to the nation's geography. His army was defeated at the Battle of Pelusium by the combined

Persian armies. He didn't have the best generals. He was too confident in his command and his troops were out-maneuvered 343 BC by the Greek generals of mercenary. After his defeat Nectanebo left Memphis and the forts of Memphis protected the walled towns. These forts, made up of Greek and Egyptian warlords, were susceptible to jealousies and suspicions from the Persian authorities. Therefore, the Persians were quickly able to lower many towns across Lower Egypt. They were also on their way towards capturing Memphis when Nectanebo pulled away to Ethiopia. The Persian army defeated Nectanebo's army and took over the Lower Delta of Nile. Artaxerxes became the ruler of Egypt, after Nectanebo had fled to Ethiopia. The Jews deported from Egypt to Babylon or south coast Caspian Sea were the Jews of Phoenicia.

Artaxerxes conquered the Egyptians. He destroyed the city walls, established a rule to fear, and robbed all temples. Persia was able to gain a great deal of wealth through this plunder. Artaxerxes raised taxes and attempted to compromise Egypt until it was no longer insurgence against Persia. Persia overthrew Egypt's original faith followers, who were mistreated. During this time, valuable texts were taken. Before returning to Persia in 1821, he created Pherendares as the satrap of Egypt. Artaxerxes was able extravagantly to compensate his mercenaries from the gold he gained during his reconquest in Egypt. He left Egypt after his intrusion was complete and returned to his capital.

Artaxerxes conquered Egypt. He returned to Persia, where he spent the next few months stopping all revolts in various areas of the Empire. Thus, the Persian Empire was established under his rule within a few short years. Egypt belonged to the Persian Empire, until Alexander The Great conquered it.

After the conquest in Egypt, there was no further rebellion or disobedience against Artaxerxes. Bagoas and coach, the 2 generals who had stood out the most during the Egyptian project were promoted to high-ranking roles. Coach, as the ruler of all the Asiatic coasts, was able to suppress many chiefs who had rebelled against Persian rule during the current turmoils. The entire Asian Mediterranean coast was brought under Coach's control and made dependent in just a few short years.

Bagoas returned from the Persian capital with Artaxerxes. There he played a crucial role in the empire's internal administration. And he ensured peace throughout the Empire. Over the last six years of Artaxerxes' reign, the Persian

Empire had a strong and efficient federal government.

Lycian, Ionian, and Lycian warriors gained control of the Aegean- and Mediterranean Seas as well as much of Athens' 2,000 year old isle empire. Isocrates began giving speeches to demand a crusade versus the barbarians', but none the Greek city-states had the strength to meet his demands.

Despite there being no revolts in the Persian Empire, Artaxerxes found himself drawn to Macedon by Philip II. He was aware of Macedon's growing authority and terrain. Demosthenes had already warned the Athenians. The Persian impact was to be used to constrain and control the Macedonian empire's power and increasing impact. A Persian force was dispatched to Cersobleptes in Thracia, to protect his liberty in 340 BC. Philip's huge and fully-equipped army that had been leading his siege on Perinthus was defeated by the city of Perinthus. Philip II had devised strategies to infiltrate the Persian Empire. His profession would be celebrated by Artaxerxes' death, but the Greeks refused their support.

Bagoas poisoned Artaxerxes using the assistance of a doctor in 338 BC.

Chapter 5: Why the Empire Fails

Artaxerxes II Arses altered Artaxerxes' third, before he could do anything. Bagoas is also said to have killed Arses and his offspring as well as many of the land's princes. Bagoas also placed Artaxerxes V's nephew Darius III, Artaxerxes III, on the throne. Bagoas was forced into taking in toxin from Darius III (the previous Satraps of Armenia). Alexander and his battle-hardened soldiers attacked Asia Minor in 334 BC as Darius was about retaking Egypt.

Alexander the Great (Alexander the Third Macedonian) defeated the Persian troops at Granicus (334 BC), Issus (2333 BC), Gaugamela (330 BC) In the beginning of 330 BC, Alexander made progress on Susa and Persepolis. Both were defeated. Alexander traveled north to Pasargadae from Persepolis. Here he found the burial ground of Cyrus. This is the place where Cyrus was buried, the tomb of the

Cyropedia man that Alexander had examined.

Alexander's intrusion into Persia resulted in the destruction of Cyrus' burial place and ransacked the majority of its riches. Alexander found the burial spot and was shocked by the disrepair. He asked the Magi for their help, and they were put on trial. Alexander brought the Magi to trial more as a way to protect Cyrus' burial spot than as a means to show his may and degrade their impact. Alexander the Great ordered Aristobulus's restoration of the burial spot's interior to improve its condition in a token of his respect for Cyrus. He then headed to Ecbatana. There, Darius the Third was taken refuge.

Bessus III's Bactrian servant and kinsman, was able to abduct him. Alexander was nearing, Bessus had his men assassinate Darius III and then declare himself Artaxerxes IV, Darius III's heir. Alexander was postponed by Bessus who then carried Darius' body to Persepolis to be properly buried. Bessus then formed a union with his men to make an army capable of defeating Alexander. Alexander found Bessus in Persia and put him on trial.

Alexander maintained the Achaemenid governmental structures, earning him the name "the final of the Achaemenids," according to certain scientists.

Alexander's empire split between his generals the Diadochi after his death 323 BC. This led to some small nations. Alexander's general SeleucusI Nicator was responsible for the Seleucid empire, which was the largest and most well-controlled across the Iranian plateau. The Parthians of northeastern Iran would return native Iranian control during the second century BC.

The substantial tax burden of the state, which led to financial collapse, was partly responsible for the decline in Empire.

It was estimated that the countries in question would pay $180 millions each year in tribute. This doesn't include tax payments or material products. This money was used to fund the regal treasure after the excessive overhead of the federal government--the army, the administration, and any other satraps who could easily dip into the coffers. Diodorus states that Alexander the Third discovered 180,000 Attic skills of sterling at Persepolis. The Macedonians also had additional treasure, which Parmenion at Damascus had already found. This amount was worth $2.7 million in the United States. Darius The Third had also taken 8,000 talents with him on his voyage to the north. Alexander rebuilt the economy's fixed stockpile, and by the end of his life, 130,000 skill points had been spent on building cities, dockyards, temples and troop payment in addition to regular federal government expenses. Harpalus the satrap had also left Greece with 6,000 talents, which Athens used for rebuilding its economy following the battles of the Corinthian League.

Despite that, Alexander's cash infusion into Greece caused disruptions to the economy, including banking, leas, disturbances to farming, banking, and leas. The big increase in mercenary soldiers that money afforded the rich allowed them to work with it.

Another reason the Empire died after Xerxes, was the failure to unify the numerous subject countries into a single entity. It was never able to build a national identity.

This lack cohesion caused a decrease in the effectiveness and efficiency of the armed forces.

Chapter 6: Cultural Factors In Society

The Persians were greeted to huge birthday feasts (Herodotus 8), and then they would enjoy a lot of desserts. He also noticed that Persians loved red wine. It was used for guidance and thought, allowing them to think about their worries when they were drunk, then making a decision on whether to make a decision the next morning when they are sober. Alexander the Great taught Persians to bow before their superiors and kings.

Faith

Spiritual tolerance is a characteristic of the Achaemenid Empire.

According to The Old Testament, King Cyrus The Great released the Jews of Babylonian captivity between 539 and 530 BC. He allowed them to return to their homeland.

Cyrus, the Great, assisted with the repair of some towns' spiritual sanctuaries.

Zoroastrianism came to South-Western Iran in the Achaemenid-dynasty. There, it was adopted and made a specific part of Persian society. The religious belief not just codified the concepts of the gods and deities in the Iranian temples but also included original concepts such as the concept of free choice.

Zoroastrianism grew during the empire's rule under the patronage Achaemenid emperors. By the fifth Century BC, it was the most common state religion.

Herodotus indicated the time period between Artaxerxes 1 and Darius 2" The Persians don't have god images, temples or altars and view their use as absurd. This belief is due to the fact that gods don't have the same nature or attributes as men. He wrote that the Persians offered sacrifices to: "the sun, the moon, earth, fire, water, wind, and the sea." These are the only gods that have received praise since the beginning. They began to praise Urania later, which they learned more from the Assyrians as well as the Arabians. According to the Persians, Anahita and Mylitta are the names of this goddess. (The original name was Mithra. The mix-up Anahita/Mithra has been clarified. Both were worshipped in the exact same temple.).

Berosus, a Babylonian scholar/priest, wrote almost seventy year after Artaxerxes II Mnemon's rule.

Berosus also backs Herodotus in claiming that the Persians didn't know about divine being images until Artaxerxes 2 erected them. Herodotus speaks out about the sacrifice techniques, writing that "they raise no altar, set no fire, and put no libations." This sentence can be understood to mean a significant, but later, Zoroastrian accretion. While the Yasna Rite, which includes the putting libations and a wooden-burning altar, is certainly connected to modern Zoroastrianism in the late-5th century, it was not yet developed. Boyce also refers to this development as Artaxerxes II ruling in the fourth century BC, which is an orthodox reaction against the development and growth of shrine cults.

Herodotus explained that "no prayer or offering can take place without a magistrate present," though this should not necessarily be used in the same way as what is now called a magus. A magus is a Zoroastrian priest named a modupat (contemporary Persian : mobed). It is unclear if Herodotus' use the expression as one the Medes' castes or tribes suggests that these magi are Medians. They were essentially a genetic priesthood, spread throughout Western Iran. Though initially unaffiliated with any religion, they were generally in charge for all routines and spiritual activities. Although Zoroastrianism saw the magus as a later association (Sassanid era, 3rd--7th Century AD), it was Herodotus who in the middle of the 5th century brought Zoroastrianism doctrinal adjustments. These are considered cancellations to the prophet's original theories. Herodotus had practiced many of these routine acts, including the revealing of dead.

Women's Contribution

The Achaemenid Empire had a different status for women depending on their origin. Persia's status of Persian women in real Persia was generally determined by mythological Scriptural guidelines and at times prejudicial Ancient Greek resources. The best reference is the archeological Persepolis Stronghold Tablets. (PFT) defines women in connection to the regal Court in Persepolis.

The king's mom was at top of the magnificent women's hierarchy in Persian court. Next came the queen and the monarch's daughters. Finally, the king's courtesans and other women of regal palace.

The king was usually married to a Persian noblewoman or a nobleman from the noble family. While members of the powerful family can wed loved ones, there is no record of any marriage between half-siblings. The courtesans of a king included servants, detainees in certain cases, or foreign princesses. These were all immigrants and were not permitted to wed the king.

Although the Persian court has no archeological evidence, it seems that the emperor kept many courtesans within a Hareem.

The imperial wives ate breakfast and supper together with the King and accompanied him during his journeys.

They could have joined in the imperial hunt or regal banquets. Herodotos describes how Persian envoys to Macedonian required the participation of women at a supper, because it was popular for girls from their own country to be able to partake in banquets.

The archeological evidence indicates that the queen was present at the time the king addressed his audience. Noblewomen and noblewomen can travel alone and may be accompanied by male or female attendants. They are also able to own and manage their own fortune, land and business. Long capes and veil worn by

Persian girls do not cover their hair or hide their faces. They are instead draped over their necks as decoration.

Royal and noble Achaemenid wives were taught in courses like archery and horsemanship, which weren't compatible with privacies.

Royal and glamorous women owned and managed vast estates and workshops. They also used a variety of skilled workers and servants.

Not least the primary spouse was a magnificent or noble man. This is because partners were often present with their spouses at supper tables, but they left the table when the "women performers" arrived and the men took their seats.

While the Achaemenid Emperor was not governed by any woman as queen or regent in its early days, certain queens, including Atossa (and Parysatis) are well-known to have had an influence on state affairs.

However, although there is no evidence of women serving as spiritual or administrative leaders, archeological evidence suggests that Persepolis had many women who worked for free alongside men.

Women could work as leaders of their labor workforce, which is known as arraara panena. These workers were paid more than their male counterparts. Certified workers within the crafts, however, were paid the same regardless of gender.

O. Mustafin's image of the Tomb of ArtaxerxesIII

On closer inspection, we found several figures in the rock face. These figures appear to be mourning the death of their Emperor, as shown by the cross-shaped incisions that have been carved into the rock. Each one has an entrance far above the ground. This is also where Darius I, Xerxes and Artaxerxes I were buried. The majority of these were in stone sarcophagi. In the tomb of Artaxerxes I, Kings Artaxerxes III and Darius III may have been buried.

All six tombs are identical in form and design. It is believed that they were all copied from Darius II's. They also share a resemblance to the Tachara's carving facade. In the tomb register, the king appears to be standing on a platform supported by his servants. Bas-reliefs showing the Persian king giving sacrifices to Ahura Mazda and a flame are depicted on these tombs. A well-preserved basin of water is located just in front the tomb of Darius II. This water basin was believed to be used in funeral ceremonies. [83]

Persepolis was the place where Persian kings managed the vast empire. This is a unique way to think about how an empire should be run. Contrary the common consensus in ancient history, where cultures were determined to conquer, obliterate, then rebuild their empires according to their terms, Persia was not like that. Persia sought political objectives through tolerance and respect for cultural diversity. To continue living according their own cultural and customs, the subjects nations only had to pay their taxes.

To avoid confusion and babble, an old Persian language was used during ceremonies and other official acts. They once again demonstrated their desire to create a common world in which all people could live. Old Persian was used by the Persian bureaucracy as the official language. This was a crucial step in the transition from an empire that included many different peoples to a single state. [84]

The Persian view of the empire being multifaceted was strikingly different from the imperial precedents their forebears had. The Assyrian Empires' subjects had previously spoken and written several languages. However, when it came time to inscribe palaces or monuments of rulers with inscriptions, they were the ones who wrote them. Thus, the identity of an empire was defined in terms of its rulers. The Achaemenid languages, on the other hand, were extraordinary symbols of the relationships of rulers and ruled. They were presented in both the Old Persian language (the official one) and the languages their vassal states, Elamite or Akkadian. [85]

The Persians gave freedom to subject nations, ensuring that the multiethnic and multilingual empire prospered in relative peace over 250 years. To maintain control over territory stretching nearly 3,000 miles, it required more than tolerance. In order to keep control, empires need infrastructure.

An ancient Persian road leads to Persepolis and is found 50 miles away from Persepolis. The road was built into a hillside, with sides up to 30 ft high. [86] These engineering feats were repeated across the empire. Persians had a network roads and highways that allowed them to move information, people, and material from one part of the empire to another. The Persian road system that ran from Persepolis and Susa to Ecbatana via Pasargadae to Ephesus in the Mediterranean was impressive enough to impress even the Greeks. [87] Other roads ran east to India. These roads also brought information to Persepolis from the Persian kings. This was a surprise for the Greeks. Herodotus the great Greek historian wrote that "no mortal thing can travel faster than these Persian couriers." [88]

The staging post, another Persian innovation made it possible to travel so fast. This system enabled a messenger to ride on one horse and change their horses quickly at the garrisons approximately every 20 mile along the highways. Then they could continue their journey. [89] These staging posts were also manned with Persian soldiers. They allowed traders and travellers to travel across large tracts of land in relative safety.

Through art from the city, much can be learned about the structure of imperial power and its nature. Two sculptures depicting the royal audience were found in archaeological investigations. One of these scenes is housed in the Iran National Museum. The other is located in the Persepolis Treasury. These sculptures had been originally attached to the Apadana stairways' central facade. They were later moved into the Treasury. [90] The king appoints members of his family, or his most trusted men, to take up the chosen positions. King Darius is shown seated in a canopy with several senior officials supporting him. Pharnaces is the son Arsames and chief economic official. He was responsible to pay food gifts for residents and visitors. [91] The master in ceremonies was present before the throne to report on the festivities. It is depicted as ushers introducing gift-bearing delegations and letting them in.

The exchange and reception of gifts was a central element of Persian power and ideology. This is why the Apadana was chosen as the main location. [92] So it wasn't surprising that Alexander, the Great, targeted this structure specifically to be destroyed.

One particularly fascinating inscription, found in Queen's Quarters, suggested that there may have had been competition when it came time to a ruler's succession. The inscription describes the ascendance of Xerxes onto the Persian throne, following the death Darius I. It says, "My dad Darius had other sons. But - thus Ahuramazda wanted - my father Darius made him the largest after himself. By the grace of Ahuramazda, I became king upon my father's throne when my father Darius left the throne." [93]

In 1931, the Oriental Institute of the University of Chicago began excavations at the acropolis. In 1933, fragments of tablet fragments were discovered in two rooms of the gatehouse located at the edge of the terrace's stone. These became the Persepolis Fortification Tablets. They were composed of 30,000 fragments and complete tablets. These documents provide us with one of the few resources of information about empire operations that was written by the Persians. Information that we otherwise would never have had access to. They were written with several languages. These documents were preserved together in antiquity as a treasure chest of coins and were later discovered together in modern times.

What does this tablet reveal about Persepolis and its people? They weren't about the deeds and characters or marches of armies or the eunuchs/harem intrigues or other topics that Hellenistic authors and artists were interested. They consist mainly of invoices and receipts for the empire that were created in a very short time span of 20 years. This was around 500 BC. [94] They also record one aspect about the Persian Empire: the centralization of food provision. They detail transactions involving a wide range of grains and beer, wine and animals. One of the records lists "one and half-shekels in silver for carpenters creating sculptures," while another details "one glass of wine per seventy-four Syrian laborers." [95]

They were able to build a network of trading routes across their empire. The Persians also had the luxury goods they needed to keep their elite loyal. Persepolis's perceptions of power, and the propaganda associated with kingship was what made luxury a priority. It is to possess excessive amounts of expensive clothing and have one's palace covered with textiles. This is a way of expressing power and wealth. [96]

In this vein, the Persian feast is a tradition that both amazed and terrified the Greeks. Most of what we know about the Persian feast can be found in Greek sources. The Greeks describe the extravagant objects and the extensive drinking that took place. The Persians lived by the principle of telling truth. This was something that the Greeks begrudgingly admired in them. They believed that the only way to tell the truth was to drink at feasts. [97] The act of feasting brought groups together and allowed them to share the same food as well as enjoy the same experience.

It's not surprising that the Persians were famous for their extravagant lifestyle. The evidence from archaeological records and records shows that they bought gold, purple dyes, and many of the most exquisite textiles. Even though the walls and pillars of stone are gone, Persepolis' palaces and halls were decorated in exquisite textiles. [98] These fabrics could have been used on walls, the floors, and even the furniture to indicate status. [99]

Due to its huge scale, lavish decoration, and luxurious ceremonies and events, it must have cost an inordinate amount. It is evident that the Persians were capable of affording it through state investment. They also made sure that the fertile Persian homeland prospered during the Achaemenid rule. They relied on agriculture for their income. The Persepolis Fortification Tablets confirm that grains and other produce were the main means of tax payment.

Along with the taxes and tributes they paid to their vassals, the Persian royals also benefited from the extensive trade between their realm and other countries along the land-based Silk Road routes and via the Persian Gulf maritime trade routes. They often served as middlemen for transactions between their neighbors due to their position. Their economy relied on a system that used standardized coinage. They also had a form banking system that made it possible to make the market more secure. [100]

The gift giving was an important way that the Persian monarchs reinforced their subjects' loyalty. However, there were other, less benign ways they could exercise their power. Bas-reliefs at Behistun (northwestern Iran) show the Persian king in his most brutal form. King Darius the Great can be seen inflicting slavery on those who are threatening his throne. [101] Many ancient Greek records also mention that the Persians ruled by an iron fist. This includes descriptions of how the Persians severed the noses, limbs, and heads of their prisoners.

Persepolis bas-reliefs, however, offer a unique perspective. These figures are not rigidly imposed by courts or enslaved. Instead they are relaxed and encourage one another. They are shown as holding hands and shoulder to one another, creating a picture of harmony and peace. There are no battle scenes in the city and there is no violence. The Achaemenid Kings were patient, peaceful, and wealthy.

The First Persian War

500 BCE. Athens and Sparta were the two major Greek cities-states. They were not interested in the affairs or the Achaemenid Persian Imperial Empire. For the most part, they were unaware of the status of Ionian Greeks. Sparta was at the top of an alliance/league Peloponnesian state-states more concerned with the region. Athens was just learning how democratic government works (Forrest 2001: 37).

Athens remained uninvolved. Perhaps following the lead of their Athenian relatives, some of the Anatolian Ionian, Aeolian or Doric city states rebelled against their own tyrants. Herodotus gives the best account about the Ionian Revolt. It was mostly instigated and led by Aristagoras a former ruler who believed a successful revolt would put him in a strong position. Herodotus wrote that certain substantial citizens of Naxos were forced by the people to flee the island. They fled to Miletus where they found refuge under Aristagoras the son of Molpagoras. He was Histiaeus' nephew, and his son-in-law, Lysagoras' son. . . After they arrived they asked Aristagoras to lend some troops to them in hopes of regaining their home. Aristagoras was convinced that if the exiles returned, he would also be ruler of Naxos. So he offered to lend them troops.

Aristagoras had both a keen sense for politics and a feeling for the times. As part of his strategy, Aristagoras promised the Ionians Greeks the reward of democracy. He had to abdicate the tyranny of his own, which he did in public. Herodotus states that to persuade the Milesians, he began with claiming to abdicate tyranny in favor a popular government. Then, he continued the same thing in the other Ionian state, where he removed the tyrants. (Herodotus in The Histories. V, 37).

Aristagoras realized that convincing the Ionian States to rebel was not enough to defeat the Achaemenid Empire. He would need support from one, or both, his mainland Greek Greek cousins to do this. Aristagoras failed to secure the help of Sparta as well as Athens in their fight against the Persians. It would also lead to his death. The Athenians would then embark on a crash course to the Persians, which would culminate at Marathon.

A map showing the huge extent of Achaemenid Imperialism

Aristagoras visited Sparta initially to appeal for assistance against Persians.

Sparta was then governed by a republican monarchy. Only adult males could vote at the councils. Two kings ruled the city and made decisions about state affairs like diplomacy and war. Cleomenes became the sole reigning monarch of Sparta when Aristagoras made it there. Cleomenes tried to appeal initially to Aristagoras' patriotism but then his pride and finally his greed. Herodotus recounts Aristagoras' plea to Cleomenes. He says, "I trust Cleomenes, I hope that you won't be too surprised by my anxiety to visit. These are the circumstances. These are the circumstances. That Ionians should have been forced to work as slaves for free men is a grave shame on us and the rest Greece. It is also a huge loss to you, who are leaders in the Greek world. We appeal to you in the name the gods Greece to spare your Ionian cousins from being slaves. It won't be easy, as the foreigners aren't interested in war and your soldiers are the best in the world. The Persians use short spears and bows, while the Persians wear trousers and turbans. This will prove how easy they can be defeated! It is also home to more wealth than all of the rest of the world - it has everything, including gold, silver or bronze, intricately embroidered clothing, beasts and burdens, as well as slaves and other animals. All of these you can have if it is your wish." (Herodotus. The Histories. V, 49).

Cleomenes was interested in Aristagoras' map of the great Achaemenid Empire. Cleomenes then asked Aristagoras for a map. The Spartan replied that his proposal to make Lacedaemonians three months away from the sea was a highly inappropriate one. (Herodotus. The Histories.

Aristagoras did not seem to be bothered by the Spartans' refusal to accept his proposal. He stopped in Athens however to offer a similar proposal to the citizens. Aristagoras approached Athenians when it was a good time. The Athenians had just expelled Hippias, their tyrant who was supported by Persians so they were already inclined against them (Herodotus. The Histories. Aristagoras used many similar arguments to his Spartans encounters, such as the weakness of Persian military forces and the wealth of the Achaemenid Empire. However, he also appealed a common ancestry that Athenians were and Ionians. Herodotus stated, "In addition he pointed to the fact that Miletus has been founded by Athenian settlements, so it was only fair that the Athenians would help her in her time of need. The Athenians granted Aristagoras permission to appeal. They then passed a decree for the dispatching of twenty ships to Ionia, at the command of Melanthius. (Herodotus. The Histories., V. 97).

Athenian support of the Ionian cause was weak at best. The whole Ionian coalition fell under the power of the Achaemenid Empire. Aristagoras fled to exile after the Persians were able to establish their rule over the rebellious Ionian states. Miletus was among the cities that suffered from brutal punitive punishments. (Herodotus. The Histories. Vol. V. 126). Herodotus described graphically the punishments the Persians imposed on the Ionians.

The Achaemenid Persians' violent suppression of Ionian Revolt proved the first action in the greater Greco-Persian Wars. Although the Athenians thought their limited involvement in it would help to mitigate the fury of Persian King Darius I (ca. They were terribly mistaken. Despite their participation in the Ionian Revolt being minimal, the Athenians were at odds against the Persian emperor. This put them on an eight-year crash course that culminated at the Battle of Marathon.

Darius I depicted in ancient times

The Greek city states were equally at risk of fighting each other in the 5th century BCE. The Persians, however, were the rulers of the Achaemenid Imperium, which stretched from Bactria (presentday Afghanistan) in the east and Egypt in the West (Briant 2003: 366). Apart from possessing Egypt's ancient and venerated kingdom, the Achaemenid Pers also controlled Babylon and the Levant regions. These areas were home to many other illustrious cultures, including Israel, the Phoenicians and Assyrians. From this perspective, it is clear that the Greek Ionian state-states of Ionia were a tiny fraction of the empire. And the distant Athenians may have seemed to the Persians like minor intruders who were playing dangerous games out of their league. Despite the fact the Persians may have dismissed any military threat that Athenians posed in general, Ionia remained an important part of Achaemenid Empire.

Darius I was undoubtedly furious when the Athenians supported the Ionian Revolt. But their direct interference in Achaemenid Empire affairs was not their first offense against Persians. Before the Athenians became involved with the Ionian Revolt in the first place, they had been involved in a war between Sparta and they sought alliance with Persia when that didn't go well. To meet Artapherenes the Persian governor, the Athenians sent envoys out to Sardis in Ionia. They requested that the Greeks present a symbolic gift of water and earth to him. Herodotus explained, "To strengthen our position, we sent representatives to Sardis with the intention of concluding an alliance with Persia. Artapherenes (son of Hystaspes), the governor, asked who the representatives of Athenians were to seek an alliance with Persia. After being informed, he concluded that the Persian case was well-examined by noting that if the Persians would signify their acceptance by the usual gifts of earth and waters, then Darius would be willing to make a deal with them. If they did, they'd better return home. The envoys wanted to make the pact and so they accepted Artapherenes' terms. However, they were censured by Athens upon their return.

Herodotus wrote that the Athenian ambassadors were disciplined for their obeisance towards Persians. However, the political damage was already done. Athenians broke Persian tradition and protocol when offered earth and water, but they did not obey. Hippias the tyrant from Athens who was expelled in 510 CE, arrived in Sardis, and asked Artapherenes (151-52) to restore him as tyrant in Athens. Hippias actually was present with the Persian fleet at the time that the Persians invaded Greece. This suggests that the invasion was at the very least partly intended to restore Athens' tyranny. Doenges 1998.

The Athenians were able to break the Persian political protocol. Darius I became personally involved in the matter after they supported Ionian Revolt. The Ionian Revolt did not end with the atrocities committed by the Persians. A combined force consisting of Ionian Greeks as well as Athenians seized and pillaged the city and destroyed its temple. Darius I burst into flames when he discovered the Athenians were involved in the sacking Sardis. Herodotus tells us that Darius I didn't think much of the Ionians after learning about the disaster. He asked them who they were, then called for his weapon. He took it and set it on the string. Then, he shouted, "Grant O God, that the Athenians be punished." (Herodotus. The Histories. V, 105).

Darius I was able to settle the matter: the Athenians need to be taught and brought under Achaemenid Empire's tutelage. However, the planning of large-scale military operations in ancient history required a lot of resources and time. The Persian invasion against Greece was no exception. Darius I was capable of taking on this challenge, even though the Achaemenid heart was thousands of kilometers away from Greece. Mardonius, the Persian general, was in charge of the army. He mobilized his forces in Ionia, on both land and sea, in 491 BCE. This expedition into Greece would be the most extensive military expedition ever undertaken. It was more likely that it was intended to subjugate Athens, as well as the entire country of Greece.

Mardonius, a Persian general, led his army along the Aegean coastline north from Ionia to march through Thrace and Macedonia. They were confronted by a severe storm, which destroyed all their ships. (Herodotus. The Histories. VI, 44). Although the Persian fleet was destroyed, it was only a temporary setback. The Achaemenid Emperor was able create a new army under the command of Datis. Darius I had Datis ordered to "reduce Athens or Eretria into slavery and to bring all the slaves before him." (Herodotus. The Histories. VI. 94).

Datis had many advantages compared to the Greeks. His naval superiority was overwhelming and he also had the military intelligence that Hippias, the former Athens tyrant, at his disposal (Doenges 1998). Instead of following Mardonius's route through the Aegean in the previous year, Datis led a Persian army of ships across the Aegean. Delos was reduced to slavery by Datis (Herodotus. The Histories. VI. 95-98).

Datis (and the Persians) arrived in Greece to set their sights first on Eretria. Herodotus states that the Eretrians geared up for a long siege. However, they were betrayed at the hands of some of their own citizens: "The Eretrians didn't intend to surrender their defenses to the enemy; their concern (the proposal not abandoning the town having been carried), was to defend their walls. . . On the seventh of July, Euphorbus the son Alcimachus was killed and Philagrus a son of Cyneas were the two most prominent Eretrians to betray the town. The Persians entered the town, stripped the temples and set them ablaze as revenge for the Sardis' temples.

Datis saw Eretria reduced in rubble and decided to turn his attention southward to Attica peninsula and Athens. The Athenians, however, would be better equipped and leave Athens to meet up with the Persians on the plain close to Marathon.

Athens, although a large city-state, was not a great fit for the Hellenic world. Athens remained formidable. All Athenian citizens aged between 18 and 42 were eligible for military duty (Sage 1996. 38). The army was also sub-divided in to tribes by lieutenants, known as taxiarchs (Sage 1997. 38). It is not known much about the training of men, although the Athenian military's basic structure is known. There is no evidence of formal training of hoplites in Athens during Battle of Marathon. Sparta, the only Greek city state where significant training is documented, is the only one (Sage 1996. 35). The Athenian military of the Battle of Marathon, therefore, was a "home guard," in which each citizen was responsible for his role militarily and prepared for war.

Herodotus has the most complete source about the Battle of Marathon. Other sources, however, exist that could be helpful in addition to Herodotus. The oldest known sources of information on the Battle of Marathon were actually a set of photographs painted in the Poecile Stoa about 460 BCE. This was around 30 years after that battle (Hammond, 1968, 26). Unfortunately, the photos are no longer available. But Pausanias, a Greek geographer of Greece, provided a partial description in a geographic survey of Greece. "In this place, neither side has won the better. But the middle of fighting shows the foreigners fleeing and pushing one another into a morass. The Greeks are killing the foreigners who try to enter them." (Pausanias. Descriptions of Greece. I, 5.3). Pausanias' description for the Poecile Stoa proves Herodotus' account, namely that the Plataeans were only other Greeks who fought with the Persians. It also points out the chaos created by the Persians retreat.

The Battle of Marathon was fought in September 490 BCE (Hammond 1967). Doenges 1998, 4, also believes that this battle was the first amphibious combat in world history. The Persians placed their invasion force near Marathon to allow them to maneuver their cavalry. This was what Datis, the Persian commander, believed would give him an edge over the Greek hoplites. Hammond 1968, 33. Although the Persians chose Marathon as a good spot for cavalry, the proximity of Eretria played an important role. Herodotus wrote that Marathon was the Attic territory near Eretria. This area is also where cavalry could maneuver best. Hippias son of Pisistratus led the invasion army. Athenians ran to Marathon as soon as they heard the news. The Athenian forces were commanded by ten generals, Miltiades being their tenth." (Herodotus. The Histories. VI 102-103

Marathon: Disposition

Hippias the ex-Athenian tyrant is also important as he provided intelligence to Datis (and the Persians) that made Marathon the most suitable place for cavalry operations. It was also located near Eretria. The Persians could benefit from the proximity of Eretria if they needed to conquer Attica, possibly even Greece. Because the Persian army wasn't close to the Achaemenid colonies in Ionia, it was forced to use Eretria as their temporary base and supply source (Hammond 1968. 32). For the Persians, the safe and fast route to move goods or men across the bay from Marathon to Eretria was also possible.

The Persians then assembled their army in Marathon. But the precise size of this army remains a mystery. Herodotus does not provide a figure for the Persian combatants - they only refer to the ships. So historians today are left with no other options but to estimate the size of the field, Herodotus' death toll, and the number Persian ships. A recent study suggests that the Persian army may have had between 12,000 and 5,000 fighting men (Doenges 1998. 6). However, Hammond's earlier studies put the total number at 90.000. Hammond, however, noted that many of these men would have been sailors (Hammond, 1968, 33).

Although the numbers are important, both sides fought in a completely new way. This was something that each side had mastered over decades, if not centuries, in their respective war zones. The Persian army was made of contingents that were drawn from the farthest parts of the empire. While one might expect a multinational force to adopt different styles of fighting it was actually uniform in its equipment, ancient historians who wrote about battle reveal this. It is possible, however, that the ancient Greek historians who wrote the battle described the battle as assuming all Persian units would have nearly the same equipment, as for the Greek soldiers. The Persian army which faced the Spartans at Thermopylae and their Greek allies was made up of cavalry, infantry, and chariot troops, with each one apparently being equipped in a similar manner. Military historians classified the infantry as "light", meaning that they didn't have heavy armor and weapons. Each Persian infantryman was equipped with a single, light thrusting spear (which could also have been thrown if required), a shortsword/saber as well as a double-curved bow and a shield. The shield size may have been different from unit to unit. However, archaeological evidence from Persian sculpture suggests that the shields would cover soldiers knee-to-neck while not being broad enough to make significant overlap with those on either side.

It might seem odd to use wicker for a shield, but it was actually very effective. The wicker was lightweight and very easy to carry. It was also very effective at stopping slashes by light weapons. Wicker could also trap thrust weaponry that entered it, making them difficult or impossible to withdraw. The charioteers as well as the cavalry had similar equipment. They were equipped using longer curved blades for slashing, double curved bows and javelins. Some units, especially those of the Persian heartland had double-headed, dangerous weapons, making them the Persian shock forces.

Armor for Persian soldiers also appears to have been quite standard. This is because the armor was almost non-existent in most of Persian infantry. Even though it's hard to believe, considering the Persians were facing heavily armored hoplites. However, Persian soldiers seem to have been without greaves, vambraces, or any other form arm or leg protection. Many units seem to have given up helmets and worn knotted, rags over their heads, or light caps made of metal or leather. They wore either no armor at all or light back-and breasts made of leather, metal mail or bronze scales to protect the torsos. Although the Persian elite infantry, a group of soldiers from the Persian heartlands, was more heavily armored than other units, such as the famous "Immortals", the personal guard of the

Emperor that numbered 10,000, were not generally protected.

There are two reasons why this equipment is so light: apart from the massive cost of equipping such an army like the Persians, and the fact that they were not designed to withstand the harsh climate in which the Persian army was operating most of its operations, The desert plains and mountains of Asia Minor and Egypt and the Hindu Kush's near-impassible mountains, along with the heat of the Punjab, were not ideal terrains for heavy iron steel and bronze armor. This weighed soldiers down, and might have caused heatstroke or fatigue. Accordingly, the Persian strategy was to fire arrows and javelins at their opponents from a distance. After that, they would close in on the weaker troops and then cut them with their short swords. Charioteers and cavalry would most likely also fight in a similar way to the West's Napoleonic battlefields or knee-to-knee heavy horse cavalry charges of the middle ages.

The Greeks, on the other hand, fought in a totally different way. First, many Persian soldiers were conscripts. The exception being the Immortals, which was an elite corps with the most prestigious honors in the Persian Empire, the Immortals service in which was the highest honor, but all of the Greek Infantrymen were volunteers and, generally, better-trained. Each city-state required its residents to engage in bi-annual or annual city-wide military exercises. Spartans, which were the backbone for the Greek force, spent their entire lives training and preparing to fight. Their serfs, the Helots, did manual labor. Although it isn't entirely clear why Sparta put so much emphasis on a militaristic culture, it did result in Spartans becoming obsessed with military fitness from birth.

Spartan babies who were born with slight physical disabilities were left to die. Those who were able to join the military began their training at the tender age of seven. Every Spartan male needed to be 18 years old in order to join the army.

This is why the citizen-soldier was at the heart of the Greek way for war. Except for Boeotia, most armies were almost entirely made up of infantry, with some exceptions. Even though this may sound disadvantageous against other forces like archers or horses, the Greeks were not limited to using infantry. Their greatest strength was the hoplite, a soldier who is about as different from his Persian counterpart as possible.

Most historians believe that in Greece, the hoplite was the dominant infantry soldiers around the 8th-century B.C. Hoplites purchased their own equipment. While not all hoplites would have been equally equipped, considering the nature and style of warfare, this was a necessity.

Hoplites, just like the Persian infantry carried spears. The Persian weapons were small and light while the Greek spears were longer and thicker. These spears were 9 inches tall and featured a spearhead at the top. The bottom had a "lizard-sticker" buttspike that could be used to either hold the spear upright or to replace the main weapon. A shortsword was also carried by each hoplite, which was designed to thrust in close quarters of a melee. The Spartan weapon the xiphos was only a half-inch long and its blade was barely over a meter long. The hoplites did away with bows, as opposed to the Persian infantry. The Greeks did have light infantry such as javeliners, archers and slingers. However, this role was secondary to that played by the heavy infantry.

This was due to the armor the hoplites wore into battle. The armor consisted of bronze graves covering the wearer's ankles and knees, a leather skirt or quilted lining to protect the groin region, and a breastplate either made of bronze, quilted linen, with overlapping bronze scalings. Hoplites wore a helmet to protect their heads. This helmet was made of full-face bronze and featured high-flaring cheek-pieces. A thick nasal protected their faces. It was also topped with a horsehair crown that increased their height. Line infantry wore helmets front-to back, while officers wore them sideways to be more easily recognizable by their troops during the heat of battle.

His hoplite was a well-equipped tank, with iron and brass armor from head to feet. However, his shield was the most important part of his equipment. The hoplon or Aspis, which weighed in at 30+

pounds, was a huge wooden bowl measuring over 3 feet in diameter. It was made out of heavy oak fronted in bronze. It covered each hoplite's knees and necks, as well providing significant overlap with their shields. These armaments didn't lend themselves to the Persian fighting style. It was impossible to engage an enemy from a distance when the Greek hoplites were carrying short swords, thrusting spears, or even standing still.

Greek art depicting hoplites fighting

19th century illustration showing a Hoplite

Hoplites in Greece were only as strong or weaker than the hoplites next to them. This meant that both flanks could be exposed and heavy infantry units would not move if there weren't hoplites along their sides. The Greeks introduced the phalanx, one of the most important military innovations of modern history.

The phalanx formed a line of infantry that was as long as the battlefield required, and could be anywhere from five to 30 soldiers deep. Each rank was officered in turn by a veteran. To maintain the formation's cohesiveness, there was an additional, expert file closer at each file's back.

The phalanx moved slowly to maintain its tight formation. They then speeded up in unison before entering combat. The large hoplite shields extended out in an impressive overlap, creating a wall of oak, bronze, and bronze. The first rank held their shields high, and used their swords to strike at the enemy. The ranks below the first rank would then use their spears to cut through the enemies. Each soldier's right flank was protected by his companion's sword (all shields were secured to the left side of the formation to maintain integrity). In order to counter this tendency, the phalanx, especially for less-trained units had the tendency to edge towards the right. The Greeks responded by positioning their elite soldiers to the right to provide a buffer. The rows at the back of each line would use their shields to hold the hoplites up and keep them balanced. The formation and attack strategy were meant to physically intimidate and overpower the enemy, which in turn would lower their morale. Although the phalanx fell out of favor as a combat unit at the height of Roman Empire, its principles remained applicable to subsequent infantry formations well into the American Civil War. In the gunpowder age, infantry units relied on concentrated firepower to stun and scare their enemies. The Greeks relied heavily on the hoplite as a defense unit. And military commanders discovered over and over that soldiers flee when they aren't crowded shoulder-to-shoulder in tight formations.

Although there is some disagreement on this point, many agree that the main strength for the hoplites was their inexorability when they operated as a cohesive unit, perfectly drilled. They were an unstoppable force which relied less heavily on the initial clashing shield-walls (hoplites never advanced at any run to preserve their formation) but on the relentless pushing force of moving forward to shatter enemy formations.

The Athenians faced two choices: either they would prepare the city's defenses in preparation for a siege, and/or wait for help from other Greeks such as the Spartans to arrive. Other options included meeting the larger Persian army on the battlefield close to Marathon. Both arguments were valid and both sides were heard. However the final decision was made by Miltiades to meet the Persians at the battlefield. . . Miltiades, then, was turned to Callimachus. Callimachus answered, "It is now yours, Callimachus." He said, "Either to enslave Athens. or to make her free. To leave behind you, for all future generations, a history more glorious than Harmodius, Aristogeiton, and so forth." Never before in Athenians' history has there been such peril. Hippias will take power if the Persians submit. It is obvious what misery this will bring. But if the Persians are defeated, then our city may be the most prominent among the Greek cities. . . Miltiades' words prevailed. Callimachus the war Archon voted in favor of fighting." (Herodotus. The Histories. VI.109-110).

Athenians then decided to meet the Persians in battle. Most people believe that they followed the northern route (25 miles) from Athens to Marathon (Doegnes 1997, 7). Doegnes, 1998, 7, said that the only other route to Marathon was 28 miles long and would have exposed the Greeks to a cavalry strike. The Greeks arrived in Greece and faced off against each other for a few more days. This calm helped the Greeks strengthen their forces, as well as better prepare for battle.

Once the Greeks reached the plain, they camped on a spot considered sacred to Hercules. They were then joined the Plataean Greek contingent. Herodotus states that the Athenian troops arrived on the plain at a spot considered sacred to Heracles. Then, they were joined by Plataeans who came to support them with all of their manpower. (Herodotus. The Histories. VI, 108).

It is believed that there were around 10,000 Greeks camping on the plain at Marathon. About 1,000 of these hoplites were Plataeans (Hammond 1967, 34). A majority of the Athenian Hoplites traveled to Marathon in order to confront the

Persians. A small skeleton crew, however, remained behind at Athens to defend it in case the Persian forces attacked. (Hammond68, 34).

Datis was eager to fight the Persians. They had the advantage in numbers and cavalry. The Greeks however were still making preparations to give them the best chance. The Greeks may have gradually advanced their position by cutting down trees, then using the trees to block the Persian cavalry in the days prior to the actual battle (Hammond, 1968, 39). The Greeks advanced to the actual battlefield by then, and they attempted to protect their rear and flanks from the rugged hillsides. This rendered the Persian cavalry virtually ineffective (Hammond, 1968, 39). This strategy was key to the Greeks winning the battle. Because the vaunted Persian cavalry played very little role in the Battle of Marathon, the Greek hoplites had better armor and training than the average Persian soldier who wore very little armor.

Miltiades knew better than the Greeks that they had to plan and win the battle in order to defeat the Persian army. Datis relied too heavily on his cavalry, and was unwilling or unable to innovate. While the victor may have been determined by the decisions of Miltiades & Datis prior to the actual battle itself, the two sides nonetheless had to fight. This epic battle has rightfully earned its legendary reputation.

In premodern warfare, the order of battle was a standard one. The belligerent armies would line up in a shield wall (or phalanx) across from each another, and then fight with the ultimate goal to break through the enemy's line. Herodotus' description of Battle of Marathon follows this format: "When the battle came, the Athenian army moved to position for the next struggle. Callimachus commanded Callimachus the right wing – because that was Athens' standard practice. The War Archon then led the right wing. The tribes followed in their usual order. The Plataeans remained on the left wing." (Herodotus. The Histories. VI, 111).

Callimachus the Athenian field Marshal (War Archon), was placed on one the wings rather than the center of the battle. As the two armies met, they were forced to overcome their numerical inferiority. Callimachus Miltiades, Callimachus and the other Greek generals were presented with two choices: either concentrate their forces at the center (where most likely the initial Persian thrust would occur) or put the majority on the wings to protect themselves from being flanked. Herodotus states that the Greeks chose second option. Herodotus stated that "one result of Athenian troops prior to the battle was weakening of their centre by the effort to extend their line sufficiently to cover most of the Persian front; while the two wings were strong, the line in the middle was only a few tiers deep. After the preparations were made and the preliminary sacrifice proved successful, the order was given to move and the Athenians moved towards the enemy within a short distance. . . They were, as far as we know the first Greeks who charged at a run.

The most interesting and strategically important aspect of this passage, however, is the fact that the Greeks ran for the Persians. It may seem that running to meet your enemy on the battlefield could be a disadvantageous, especially as it can tire runners, but there are also some benefits. In order to fight in hand-to—hand combat, soldiers in pre-modern battles must be in good physical form. So a fast run to meet your enemy would help raise their heart rates and get them in the best possible mood for the battle. The mile or so the Greek hoplites ran across Marathon Plain to meet with the Persian army was actually a warmup for the actual battle.

Modern scholars point out that one of the Persians' advantages was lost when the Greeks sprint to meet the Persians. The Persian cavalry threat to Persians was eliminated once the two armies had become engaged. The hilly terrain protected the Greek flanks and prevented them from being pushed back (Hammond 1968.40). The Greek formations of the battleline, which were countered by numerical superiority from the Persians, would prove to be the last straw for Datis as well as his army.

The thin Greek center fell quickly after the battle began. A burial mound discovered and excavated in the modern era marks the spot where the Greek center was and where most of the Greek casualties occurred (Hammond 1968/18). Herodotus describes how the Persians conquered the center. In the center, held by the Persians and Sacae, there was an advantage for the foreigners. They were able break the Greek line and pursue fugitives inland from sea. But both the Athenians of one wing and Plataeans of the other wing were victorious. . . They joined their wings to create a single unit. Then they turned their attention toward the Persians who had broken though in the center." (Herodotus. The Histories. VI.113).

The Greek victory was achieved by the wings. In effect, they gave the Persians the center and then collapsed on their enemies from the wings. Herodotus, a man without military experience and not very well versed in military affairs was unable to mention whether the Greeks had planned this maneuver. However, logic would indicate that they did. From the way they traveled to Marathon to the place they chose to camp to the decision about sprinting to engage the Persians, every action that Miltiades, Callimachus took during the battle was meticulous and planned. It would be difficult to believe the Greek generals didn't intend to fall the wings. Hammond pointed out, "Now is it evident that the action taken by the Athenians on the wings and the Plataeans at the wings was preconcerted; for Miltiades must have anticipating the actual developments and issued orders to the effect of which the men on his wings, if victorious in combat, were to turn towards their centre, to form a line and to aid the Greek troops of centre." (Hammond 1968. 29).

Hannibal's victory against Romans at Cannae was often considered to be the most important use of a pincers attacking of this type. This feat of generalship was copied by Napoleon at Austerlitz about 2,000 years later. Hammond, however, is incorrect in stating that Callimachus, Miltiades, and Callimachus were the ones who orchestrated the pincers attack on Marathon centuries before Hannibal. Whatever the outcome, it's clear Miltiades as well as the other Greek generals supported their cause. They also planned for contingencies and helped even the odds. But, Datis was unable to capitalise on the Persians' superior numbers at the centre of the line. Their cavalry was also ineffective (Doenges 1998; 12).

Datis was aware that the Persians had lost the battle phase when the Greek flanks crashed on the Persian centre. So he directed the Persians to abandon ship and retreat. Herodotus had very little to say about the Persian retreat. The Greeks captured seven Persians-class ships, and the two Greek generals, Callimachus & Stesilaus were killed pursuing them (Herodotus. The Histories. VI 114-115). However, Pausanias fills the gaps. He said that the Persians failed retreat may have been due to them not understanding the terrain and running into marshy waters at Marathon. They fell because of their ignorance of the roads.

Datis and Persians were losing. But they weren't defeated. Datis, with his surviving army, set sail around Athens, sailing around the Attic peninsula. (Morkot 1996. 75). For the Persians to reach Athens by Marathon, the best way was on foot, and preferably horseback. However once the Greeks had defeated them at Marathon they had to sail the entire distance to Athens. At this point, victory for the

Greeks on the battlefield at Marathon was certain. But, it is possible that all would have been lost if Datis (or the Persians) could get to Athens before them. Plutarch succinctly captured what it was like for the Greeks to race back towards Athens. Aristides was, however, left behind at Marathon to guard the captives, and the booty."

Pheidippides or Phillippides is one of most famous stories about the Battle of Marathon. Pheidippides ran approximately 26 miles from Marathon to Athens, in order to notify the residents that the Greeks had won. This was according to Plutarch, the 2nd Century CE Greek writer Lucian. Lucian wrote that Phillippides (the one who served as a messenger) was regretful to have used it first. He delivered the news of victory from Marathon to Athens and addressed the magistrates, when they were anxious. He said, "Joy and you, we won." And then he went to his final breath, saying, "Joy and you!" (Lucian's A Slip of The Tongue in Greeting #3).

Darius I didn't stop his punitive actions for Athens even after the Battle Of Marathon. Herodotus states that the Persian loss in Marathon only aggrieved the Achaemenid ruler: "When Darius, son Hystaspes king of Persia received the news of Marathon, his anger towards Athens, already intense due to the assault on Sardis's head, was even greater. He was more determined than ever before to wage war upon Greece. He sent messengers to the various states he controlled with orders to create an army that was larger than it had been before and to transport warships and horses. So the royal command went round, and Asia was in turmoil for three long years. He ordered couriers to all the states under his control with orders to raise an army much larger than before. Also, he instructed warships, transports, horses, grain, and warships. The revolt in Egypt, which was conquered by Cambyses, did not help Darius' resolve to go into war against Greece and Egypt the following year." (Herodotus. The Histories. VII).

Darius never got his chance to exact vengeance against the Athenians. He died in 487 BC (Forrest 2001. 41). The Greco-Persian Wars would go on with his son and successor Xerxes. Xerxes would lead a much larger army into Greece.

Achaemenid Persian historical record does not mention the Battle of Marathon. It also doesn't mention Greco-Persian wars. This is surprising, as Persian historical tradition was inherited from ancient Near Eastern traditions which depicted the sovereign always victorious (Cameron 1983.80-81). Even if they had used more modern or Hellenic historytoriographical traditions, the Persians would have ignored Marathon's defeat because of its one-sided nature. Herodotus states that the final casualty of the battle saw 5,400 Persians die, while the Greeks lost 192 (Herodotus. The Histories. VI, 117).

The Second Persian War

Although Darius I is confirmed to have been succeeded by Xerxes I, modern scholarship is not clear on the matter. This issue is crucial when considering why the Greco-Persian Wars were initiated by the Persian king. Herodotus (The Histories. VII. 2-4) has a long description of Xerxes' accession to Darius I's throne. It was due to Atossa as the crown prince and the fact Xerxes was born when Darius I was king. His older brothers were born before he became king. Old Persian cuneiform inscriptions in Persepolis attest to Xerxes' rise up to power. "Xerxes Pesepolis a" (XPa), a text that states: "Saith Xerxes

King: Other sons Darius there were (but), - thus unto Ahuramazda the desire Darius my dad made me the greatest of all after himself. My father Darius passed away and I was made king upon Ahuramazda's throne. I did a lot of excellent (construction) when I became king. I protected the father's building and I also added other buildings." (Kent 1953, 150).

This text clearly aims at proving that the new king can rule the Achaemenid Empire. The text also reveals that Xerxes devoted at most a portion of his resources and time to building projects. This was a way that many kings in ancient Near Eastern cultures legitimized the rule of their heirs.

Given the fact that he was facing rebellions and questions about his legal right to rule, it is not surprising that Xerxes made a Herculean effort in order to invade Greece soon after his father had fallen. Herodotus explains that Xerxes was a geopolitical power who had his interests in Egypt, to the south, when he came to power 486 BCE. As Xerxes prepared to launch his punitive assault against the Egyptians the Persian general Mardonius (who was known for losing the Persian fleet at Greece during the reign Darius I) convinced the Great King also to invade Greece. Herodotus writes that Xerxes started by building an army for a campaign to Egypt. Mardonius - Marryas, the brother of Darius and Gobryas' sister - was present in court. He had more influence than anyone else in this country and used to chat to him often about the matter. He would then say to his master, "Master," that the Athenians had caused us great pain and should be punished for it. After you have dealt with Egypt's arrogance, it is possible to lead an army against Athens. Do this, and you name will be held in honor all over the globe. People will think twice before they invade your country in the future." (Herodotus' The Histories VII, 5).

Mardonius had an influence on Xerxes, as he answered the call to arms. Xerxes also received additional incentives for upholding family honor and retribution after the destruction of Sardis by the Athenians during the Ionian revolution. Xerxes declared: "I will cross the Hellespont and march a army through Europe into Greece. And punish the Athenians because of the outrage they perpetrated upon my father, and upon us." Darius, as you can see was already making preparations for war on these men. Unfortunately, his death prevented him from fulfilling his mission. As a representative of him and for the good of all my subjects I will not rest till I have taken Athens to its ground and set it ablaze, in retaliation for the insult that the Athenians had done to me and my dad without provocation. These men, you will recall, came with Aristagoras, the Milesian, to Sardis and burned the temples.

These passages both reveal Xerxes initial reluctance of attacking Greece as well as his passionate personality. However these two passages were both important in how the fighting ended up. Regardless, once the emperor favored a European invasion, the great Persian army had to be mobilized, and moved from Asia towards Europe.

The Persian army's mobilisation and mustering were without doubt the largest ever in history. They probably were the largest up to the First Crusade approximately 1,500 years later. The logistics of assembling an army took many years. Herodotus said the army required a large amount of materials. The historian stated that "For the four year following the conquest, the mustering and provision of troops and supplies continued. Towards Xerxes' fifth birthday, he was at the head his huge army and began his march. . . With other armies like them, all these armies would not have equaled Xerxes' army. There was no nation in Asia that he took with him to Greece. Aside from the great rivers was there any stream his army could drink that wasn't dry? Some nations provided ships, while others formed infantry troops; from some cavalry was ordered, from others horse transports and crews; from other, again, triremes to build floating bridges or provide provisions and craft of different kinds." (Herodotus. The Histories. VII, 20-21).

From 484-481 CE, the army assembled in Sardis. Then they set out in the spring 480 for the long trek to Greece. Before the army fled Sardis, Xerxes sent representatives through Greece to demand the symbolic water and earth from the various kingdoms. Earth and water were given as a sign of respect and obedience to the Persian ruler. In turn, the Persian ruler agreed to remove the subordinate ruler from power and to not cause any damage to his temples and people (Briant 2002). Xerxes didn't send any demand for earth or water to the Greek capitals - Athens & Sparta - as the Persian messengers were killed in the first war (Herodotus. The Histories. VI, 133). It would have been incompatible with the partly punitive aspect Xerxes' expedition to Athens to demand water. Xerxes wanted the Athenians to be subservient to him and not to be destroyed and enslaved.

Herodotus stated that the entire army (sailors, sailors and support personnel) numbered 1,700,000. Herodotus also said that it took them one week to cross and bridge the Hellespont. This is a channel in Aegean separating Asia from Europe.

Although the number is likely to have been exaggerated it is still the most important figure regarding the size and proportion of the Persian army to the Battle of Salamis. Herodotus referred to 1207 triremes as the Persian fleet. Persia, being a landlocked country was responsible for almost the entire navy. This included 300 ships that were manned with Phoenicians and 200 that were sailed to Egypt (Herodotus The Histories VII, 89–96).

Xerxes as well as the Persians weren't the only ones to prepare for the coming war. The Persian army started its long march through Europe. However, the Greeks and especially the Athenians also prepared for the eventual victory at the Battle of Salamis. Recognizing the inevitable nature of war, the Athenians had already begun to build a large fleet. However, Athens was unable to afford both the treasure and the manpower necessary for funding both a permanent army and a fleet. They had therefore sought help from elsewhere. In disregard of the 481 BC Xerxes ambassadors, the chief Greek state met at Corinth, to decide what was to happen. Their resolve was a clear indication of the severity of their crisis, as the Greek city states were notoriously fractured and only gathered in times of great need.

Xerxes was planning to cross the straits by building a huge bridge made of boats at the Hellespont. This ambitious project is the culmination of one of antiquity's most colourful legends. Herodotus stated that the Persians tried to bridge the Hellespont first, but failed due to a storm that destroyed the flax cables and the papyrus cables. Enraged, Xerxes ordered the men to whip the Hellespont using 300 lashes and to throw fetters in water.

Illustration of Xerxes' command to his men to whip Hellespont, 1909

A force of 10,000 allied forces, under the command and control of the Spartans, were sent to blockade Tempe's pass in Thessaly. They discovered that Xerxes was marching on them after the meeting at Corinth. Despite first failure, the Persians did the impossible and physically crossed the Hellespont at 480 B.C. to reach northern Greece. Tempe was waiting for them south. The Persians could only stop Xerxes by crossing the Hellespont. They would need to go through Thermopylae's mountain pass to get to Greece. This strategic site had seen its fair share combat due to its strategic importance. The Greeks could defeat Xerxes if they could keep him at Thermopylae. The allied fleet at Artemisium could also stop the Persian navy, which could prevent a bypass.

As one would expect, the Spartans were appointed to command all allied land force. Their ability to fight was due to the fact that every Spartan citizen had been taught from an early age at the cruel warrior academy of agoge. They were also trained to excel in athletics and arms, something that they were able achieve without restrictions as all manual labor was done by the helots. Spartan Hoplites were seldom defeated. The red-clad Spartan hoplites, with the Lambdas (Greek letter "L", shaped line an inverse "V", for Laekedaemon; the Spartan Heartland), stark on the shields was enough often to drive enemies away from the field.

The Greeks made their preparations as Xerxes' army advanced towards the south through Macedonia. It was a horde meant to end all hordes. History has been subject to intense debate and speculation about the size and nature of the Persian army. Many ancient accounts have reported that it destroyed entire regions of their crops and ran dry rivers. Herodotus' and other Greek sources mention a force with between a million-two and a half millions fighting men, as well as equivalent numbers of support workers. These figures are probably exaggerated by Greek propaganda and Persian misinformation. Modern scholars believe that Xerxes' army contained between 300,000 and 500,000 men. But, this number is much smaller than the current estimates, which put it at around 100,000. Even the famous Spartans would have a difficult task.

In fact, the campaign could have ended before it even began, since Xerxes' advance was too late for the Greeks. The Spartans were celebrating Carneia. It was the traditional period of peace in Laekedaemon that no armies could march during. Leonidas, one among the Spartan rulers, begged the Ephors, Spartan high Priests, for special permission to send a unit into Thermopylae. Because of these extraordinary circumstances, the Ephors gave him permission to take the King's Bodyguard, a unit consisting of three hundred men to war.

Leonidas was certain he was marching toward his death. The Delphi Oracle, which predicted that Sparta should mourn a King in order to win, was a certainty. According to ancient records, the oracle said:

"For your, wide-wayed Sparta residents,

Persian men will either demolish your grand and beautiful city or you could be exiled.

Or, if that's not possible, then the bounds must mourn a dead monarch, from Heracles's line.

He can withstand the strength of bulls, lions, or other animals but he is strong enough to withstand them all.

I declare that he will not restrain himself until he tears apart each one."

Leonidas sought to fulfill the prophecy by personally selecting 300. Each of these men had living sons to ensure their bloodlines were not extinguished. Plutarch states that Leonidas replied to Gorgo, Queene of Sparta when he left.

Statue for Leonidas

While Spartans would have created a suicide squad, the honor of being selected was undoubtedly an honor for the men who joined Leonidas. Plutarch, an ancient Roman historian captured the essence of Spartans' thinking, culture, and storytelling a story about Paedaretus who was not selected for the Three Hundred honor, which was the highest in the State. He said that Paedaretus left happy and smiling after he learned that the State could have three hundred citizens better then him.

Leonidas and his troops marched toward Thermopylae, during the summer 480 BCE. A further 600 Spartan "peers", the perioikoi were also present. These had similar rights as full-blooded Spartan citizen and had the right to employ helot servants or light infantrymen. The total number of 1,500. Along the march, the Spartans were joined by another 3,000 Hoplites from Corinth Arcadia Mantinea Tegea & Mycenae. More troops joined them as the Peloponnese crossed into Northern Greece. The Thespians sent 700 hoplites, while the Thebans had 400. The Allies reached Thermopylae with the help of the Phokians or Locrians who lived in the area to the south. They sent all 2,000 men, according to Herodotus. To support Leonidas, the Greeks had either 6,000 or

7,500 men according to Herodotus. No matter what the actual number was, the Greeks were facing an estimated half-million men. Modern historians even estimate this figure to be higher. Modern estimates indicate that the Greeks had a chance of winning 20-1. But it's more probable that 50-80 Persians would have been there for every Greek.

The Greeks who were headed towards Thermopylae realized they would be outnumbered. Therefore, they were determined not to surrender to the enemy no matter how many Xerxes might have. Plutarch summarised it well, "The Spartans used the ask about enemy, it wasn't important how numerous there were, it was where the enemy was." The Greeks did not go to Thermopylae just to die a great death.

The Greeks planned a narrow position at Thermopylae to boost their defense. This was what became known as The "Middle Gate." An ancient wall that was constructed by the Phokians still existed at the spot. It would be useful in defending the pass. Once they had surveyed this site, some of their Peloponnesian friends suggested that they should abandon Phokiss and Locris to their fate, and instead go back to the Isthmus of Corinth to call reinforcements. However Leonidas insisted that they stand at Thermopylae and not leave, due to his 2,000 Locrian troops. Leonidas' tactical and political considerations were important. Thermopylae, or "The Hot Gates", in Greek was the best location for a numerically inferior enemy (named after the hot springs which made it a sought-after resort for travellers from all over Greece). Although the geography has changed significantly over time, the original track was approximately 100 yards long and ran along the coast. To one side, the land slid away to the rocky coastline below, while to its opposite, impassable cliffs encircled the pass. The single mountain path was capable of allowing a small force to bypass Thermopylae. The Persians didn't know this, but the Greeks did. Leonidas dispatched a thousand soldiers to guard the path and he positioned the rest of the troops defensively along the narrow passage known at the Middle Gate. This was three times tightened in total, with the Phokian wall acting as a second defensive position. The narrow passage would make it impossible for Xerxes to maintain his massive advantage in numbers. Now Leonidas' men could only wait.

Leonidas, the Spartans and his allies had established their defense position at Thermopylae. The allied fleet was able to stop Artemisium and Xerxes' army arrived. In August of 408 B.C., Spartan Scouts (possibly the Skiritai light infantry of Spartan fame, who always fought along the Spartan battle-line to the left of enemy elite troops) saw a great number of armed men advancing on the Malian Gulf. There were tens, hundreds, or even thousands of armed men. Then came a great horde of camp followers, slaves, and bullocks.

Xerxes' horde could blacken the ground from horizons, and all that stood between it to Greece and six, maybe seven thousand hoplites. Xerxes did, however, not attack in one go, possibly because he was respectful of the heavy infantry from Greece. Instead, he preferred to talk. He sent an Envoy to Leonidas & the Greeks to ask them to allow him passage and promised that the Spartans would receive untold honours if they did so. Xerxes' envoy stated that the Greeks would still be free. Inclusion in the Persian Empire would imply riches and privileges for all.

Leonidas, however didn't see things that way. He and the Greek allied generals claimed that capitulation was the equivalent of slavery. At Leonidas' stubborn refusal of seeing sense, Xerxes, the envoy, grew angry at Leonidas and insisted that Spartans as well as their allies surrender their weapons. Plutarch reports that Leonidas replied with "molon Labe," which means "Come, take them."

The words molon lebe were inscribed on marble of Thermopylae's Leonidas Monument. Today, this motto is used by the Greek 1st Army Corps.

Five days passed before the Greeks waited. Xerxes, however, decided what should be done. His navy couldn't force passage through the Straits at Artemisium. He was likely to be turned around. Thermopylae's small Greek army was impossible to beat. The Persians would not have any choice but to make a stand.

Xerxes received his orders on the fifth morning after the Persian army had arrived. 5,000 archers moved into position in the direction of the Greek encampment at Phokian's wall. The battle at Thermopylae had already begun.

Leonidas ordered Spartans to lead the charge and the Greeks took up the phalanx structure across the pass. He then placed them before the wall while the Persian archers advanced to within one hundred yards. The Persians launched a huge volley of darts at them. As all good archers, it is probable that at that range, the Persians could fire three volleys with their first arrow still in the air. Soon, the Greeks found themselves under a veritable hail darts. To the Persians' utter dismay, however, the Greeks simply ignored them. The Persian's lightweight bows were very different from the compound bows or longbows of Mongols and English. These bows could cut through armor at three hundred feet. And the Greeks' thick bronze shields, helmets and armor completely protected them against the hail of arrows that, according to ancient historians, caused only a few minor flesh-wounds. Shaken, Xerxes ordered that his archers fall back and sent in his hammer blow: ten thousand officers of his best infantry. They were natives from Media and Cissia and included a number Xerxes' relatives, scions and heirs of the royal families. It was now that the Spartans could prove their worth as the best heavy infantry worldwide.

The Medes & Cissians surged forward, like a tsunami, towards the Greek positions. Here, the Spartans, Periokoi and other Peloponnesians had taken their place in the van alongside Leonidas, who was now in his 60th birthday and therefore much older than what he's been depicted as.

However, the Persians crashed against the Greek Phalanx like a tsunami. The Persians had just confronted the famous "Wall of Bronze", but these first attackers were powerless against them. Their bravery and valor are undisputed. However, their training was poor and their equipment was inadequate to the task. The Persians' spears were shorter than the Greeks, which made it difficult to reach the Greeks before they were speared. Even if they did reach contact, the Persians' lighter shields and shorter swords and spears made it difficult for them to engage the Greek hoplites. Their light spears made contact with the large, bronze-fronted, thick armor of the hoplites. They were unable to stop their sabers or short swords cutting ineffectively at the crested helmets. Also, the bronze-wrapped, shins were covered in bronze. And their light armor and wicker defenses could not prevent the heavy

Greek spears hitting them like paper and splitting the men holding them.

Despite their advantages in numbers and the number of men they put into the pass the Persians could not make headway against Greek forces. In fact, they were soon on the receiving side of Othismos. This was something the hoplites spent countless hours practicing. This was the hoplite "mass shove", when the phalanx of hoplites began pushing the Persians behind their backs and eating their line like meat-grinders. Many thousand of the Cissians, Medes, and Cissians were slaughtered. Other victims were crushed by the men or thrown off the cliffs. Herodotus states that this was done at the cost only of a few Spartan lives. The Persians suffered such terrible carnage that Xerxes (who was viewing the battle from the highest vantage points above) jumped up three times to show his concern for his men as they were being cut into pieces in the below defile. Ctesias, the Greek historian Ctesias said that the Persians first wave was "cut into ribbons" but that only two to three Spartans had died.

Even for highly trained warriors fighting in the phalanx is extremely tiring. The Spartans were unable to endure the phalanx for more than five minutes due to their need to constantly react to a thrust, strike, or slash at will. In order to maintain a steady supply of hoplites to their meat-grinder, the Greek troops rotated the units of their units (generally divided according to city of origin), in and around the battle-line. Herodotus claims that this was also an indication of the Greeks' ability to block the entire passage. The Greek soldiers had been exhausted fighting and dropped to the ground, almost dead. Helots were quick to rush to their aid. The ground had been hard-packed and dry in summer.

A lull in battle fell as the Persian forces pulled away. This gave the Greeks the chance to catch their breath and tend the small wounds, which were due to fighting in the Phalanx. Since fighting in the Phalanx Formation consisted largely of a confused, shoving brawl where weapons burst and people lunged to get spears, knives and other weapons, it's very likely that significant numbers of wounds were caused by "friendly fire", which was overly enthusiastic hoplites. Although they suffered very few casualties in the initial fighting, the Greeks were impressed at the courage displayed by the Persians. They continued to hurl themselves at phalanx formation with their own weapons and shields in an effort to disarm their foes.

The Medes & Cissians had been able to do their best, even if it was futile, and were bloodily defeated. However, Xerxes wasn't done. After the Spartans and their allies had only barely reduced his huge horde, Xerxes launched the hammer blow that he believed would end them. His famed 10,000 man crack unit the Immortals was sent in to fight troops already exhausted from the day's battle. The Immortals were not like the Cissians nor the Medes. They marched into battle in a quiet, tomblike manner (as the Spartans did), to avoid battle panic and instill fear among the enemy. The Greek hoplites got up and took off their shields to stand on their feet. The Persians were again coming.

In the Palace of Darius I, the Immortals are depicted

Much intrigue surrounds the Persians' elite Corps, even the origins of their names. Herodotus called the force "Immortals" and said that it was because the force was always 10,000 strong. Also, there was always a new member in case of a death or injury. Persia has evidence that the unit existed. But, no name was given to them. Historical historians now believe that Herodotus (or his source) mistook the Anusiya ("companions") name for Anausa .

Herodotus outlined in his Histories the extra perks that Immortals received. They were to receive the same treatment from Greeks as their counterparts earlier. Xerxes may have hoped that the proud Immortals would get short shrift from the tired Greeks. Especially since it was not the Spartans themselves who first rose up to take their place on the battle-line. The superior training and armour of the hoplites was decisive, however. Even though they were slightly heavier armored then their Mede and Cissian counterpartss, the Immortals were no match to the phalanx. They sucked the Immortals deeper into a pass by pretending to retreat and inviting the Persians chase them. Xerxes, once again, was left to watch horror as his vaunted infantry was cut to ribbons at the pass.

Finally, as darkness fell the decimated Immortals fell behind, giving the field of war to the Greeks.

Even though the night went without incident, the Greeks didn't get much rest at the start of the second day. Despite his elite shock troops failing, Xerxes still possessed tens of thousands to hundreds of thousands more completely new troops to fight the Hot Gates. Xerxes realised that Spartans, along with their allies, would be exhausted and/or hurt by wounds, making them unable to put up a vigorous resistance and launched an attack against the Phokian walls.

Yet again, Xerxes proved to be wrong. Motivated to show their strength and endurance in order to compete with the Spartans, Xerxes was wrong again. The allied Greeks performed brilliantly on the second day. Once more, the phalanx proved to have been a stronghold that could absorb any enemy damage and shrug off the Persian attacks without hesitation. The number of casualties rose as fatigue started to set in and the Greeks became slower. Numerous casualties were reported, including many Spartans. Despite their injuries and exhaustion however, the Greeks managed a pushback against the advancing Persians once again. Xerxes' men, now terrorized by the utter invincibility, returned to their encampment around midday.

It was at this crucial time, when Xerxes was pondering if only attrition could defeat the Spartans (and their allies), that he received what amounted a blessing from the gods. Ephialtes, a native from

Thracis, walked to his aid and revealed to his commanders that there was a remote mountain route through which the Persians would be able to march to Thermopylae. This would enable the Persians and their allies to defeat the defending Greek armies. Ephialtes' name would soon be branded a traitor and his name was virtually erased from Greek history. Ephialtes' name, even today in modern Greece is synonymous with traitor. In modern Greek, his name is the synonym for "nightmare".

Herodotus said that two other men were accused in the tampering of the hidden path to the Persians. Onetas (a Carystus-born son of Phanagoras) and Corydallus (a native Anticyra). Herodotus knew it was Ephialtes. This was because the Pylagorae, the Greek deputies, who were supposed to have the best means of determining the truth, did offer the reward, not for Onetas and Corydallus' heads, but for the Ephialtes from Trachis.

Xerxes does not have to force his way through the hoplites that guard the Hot Gates. He could simply outflank their guards and be seen in their front or rear. At dawn on the third day, General Mardonius led 10,000 Immortals and 10,000 Persian troops. They surprised 1,000 Phokian holites by moving up the path Ephialtes had indicated. The Phokians found themselves in a difficult situation and were unable to protect a similar defense position. They fled to a nearby hilltop where they planned to make their final stand. However, the Persians resisted the urge to keep them at bay by firing volleys of arrows as the main force moved down the path.

A Phokian runner raced in front of them, bringing Leonidas the grim news that his troops would be under siege within hours.

Leonidas, seeing the impending disaster in his face, called a meeting of war generals with his surviving commanders. Despite previous successes, all of the Greeks knew that fighting meant death. Many of the Greek generals, including Leonidas, chose to retreat over fighting. With the weight of his prophecy, Spartan army tradition, and simple tactical sense on the shoulders, he asked the other Greek contingents not to disperse but he and the Spartans decided to stand and fight. Plutarch states that Leonidas exhorted the men of his tribe to eat well as tonight's meal in Hades.

Leonidas made this decision because he wanted to save his command from being destroyed. He could prevent the slow-moving Hoplites from fleeing before Xerxes' cavalry could attack them on the vast Plains behind Thermopylae. In this way, those who wanted to fight fought to protect those who fled.

Whether it were because the Spartans were braver than the Greeks or because they saw the tactical situation, what remained of the 700 Thespians refused leave even after being ordered. The same was true for the 400 Thebans. The Spartans' Spartans accompanied helots into battle and they refused to retreat. Consequently, while the Greek majority fled the battlefield to fight the Persians and Xerxes in their battle, a mixed group of 1,700 men remained back to defend the pass.

As the dawn broke across the battlefield Xerxes made his usual morning sacrifices. Having established that the Immortals were now advancing towards what remained of the Greek forces Xerxes ordered a new wave tenkil infantry to advance against Phokian walls.

But this time, the Greeks weren't content to stay on the defense. Instead, they made a desperate, triumphant attempt to take as many enemy soldiers with them as possible. They advanced further into the path, meeting the Persians at the point where every Greek spear or sword could be used. The fight was brutal and vicious. It lasted for hours, as the Greeks inflicted destruction upon the Persian troops. However, they began to be whittled down slowly. Herodotus said that the Greeks continued to fight with swords and daggers after all their spears had been destroyed and even their buttspikes were crushed to makeling.

Leonidas was shot to death by Persian archers. At this point, a large running battle broke out between the Persians who wanted to destroy his body and the Greeks who desperately wanted to preserve it. At this point, when fighting was at its worst, two of Xerxes' own brothers were killed. However, neither side could sustain a massacre with such ferocity long. As the Immortals approached from their rear, Persians and Greeks both retreated to draw their breath. Remaining members of the Greek force then dragged their wounded and deceased to a hill nearby the Phokian walls to make one last stand.

Herodotus claimed that the Thebans made a change of heart at this point. Historians believe that the Thebans were held hostage by Thermopylae. Herodotus suggested it. It is therefore unclear why the Greeks did not take the hostages back. Some historians suggest that the Thebans left were loyal to Thermopylae. However, Herodotus writes that they "moved from their companions, with hands upraised and advanced toward the barbarians Shouting they had surrendered they advanced towards Persians, casting all their weapons aside. Many were killed either because of revenge or because they suspected that the Persians were making a trick. But the rest were eventually captured by the Persians and taken away in chains.

The drama was in its final act. The Persians surged in on the beleaguered Greeks that stood back-to-back on the hill they chose to die on. Their armor was in pieces, the shields they had were lost or long gone, while their weapons were nothing more than blunted, twisted bits of metal and sticks. Herodotus described the final scene as follows: "Here the men defended themselves to death, the ones who had swords still using them, and those resisting with their teeth and hands." Finally, furious at all his losses, Xerxes ordered their men to fall back. His archers stood in at a distant and saw the remaining Greeks be killed with a hail arrows.

After the final battle, the Greeks had lost approximately two-three thousand men. But they were able hold the pass for three full days without losing any casualties. It was a defeat but one that gave the feeling of victory. Thermopylae got so mad at Xerxes that he ignored Persian customs to honor valiant enemy warriors and had Leonidas' bodies beheaded and crucified. Even though the Greeks who stayed behind in protest at the passage by Xerxes' forces had died to the last man they would inspire the men preparing to fight the battles ahead.

Thermopylae had once been the gates to Greece. Xerxes fought with his army and navy and advanced with his army into the heartland. The allied fleet from Greece was forced to retreat from Artemisium's blockade position towards Salamis. From there, they helped ferry the Athenians onto the island. The Persian army advanced into interior and placed Boeotia (including Thespiae), under the torch before marching against Athens. Xerxes saw the city abandoned by its citizens and vented his anger at the Greeks. He set the whole city on fire, forcing Athenian citizens watch in horror as their city fell to pieces.

The campaign ended with the construction of a stone lion at Thermopylae. This was where Leonidas' last stand at Thermopylae. All of the bodies of the victims were interred, including Helot, Spartan, and Allied. Leonidas' bones were eventually returned from Sparta. They were surrounded by a plaque with the epitaph that Simonides wrote. Since then, many variations have been created, such as, "Go tell Spartans, stranger by, that we lie here, according to the laws of their laws."

While Ancient Athens is most famous for its seafaring prowess, the Athenians may never have been able become a maritime power without some lucky circumstances. While the Persian army was in Sardis gathering their troops, a large silver-rich deposit was discovered 25 miles to the east of Athens. This area would later become Laurium (Hale 2009 7). The Athenians made this serendipitous discovery, which proved to be a blessing to their economy. However the city leaders couldn't agree on how to spend the money. The majority wanted to transfer the 600,000. drachmas of silver to a dole account, but Themistocles - the great hero at the Battle for Salamis - had other ideas (Hale, 2009, 11). Themistocles advocated that the silver surplus be used to build an army, which the Athenians would then use to attack the Greek city state of Aegina. Herodotus explained that Themistocles convinced them to drop the idea. Instead of disbursing the money, they decided to use it to construct two hundred warships in order to fight Aegina. The outbreak was a saving grace for Greece. It forced Athens' to be a maritime power.

Depiction Of Themistocles

Plutarch is a historian and biographer who confirms Herodotus' story. Plutarch also provides details about Themistocles' intelligence and personality. Plutarch wrote that "In the first place" whereas the Athenians were accustomed to divide the silver mines' revenue at Laureium among themselves they did not dare to bring before the people a motion to abolish this division and to create triremes with the money to wage war against Aegina. This was the most violent war that Hellas experienced, and the islanders dominated the sea because of the sheer number of their vessels. Themistocles proved his point by making use of bitter jealousy toward Aegina, which they loved towards her, to make it easier for him to obtain the armament he wanted. The result was that they constructed a hundred triremes using these moneys. They actually fought at Salamis with Xerxes with them." (Plutarch and Themistocles. IV, 1-2).

Themistocles' intelligence, oratory skills and guile persuaded other Athenian leaders. His plan saved their city from the Persians. But he also convinced them to build the type naval vessel they wanted. Themistocles predicted that the navy would be composed of light, fast triremes. They were made for ramming and didn't carry many marines (Hale, 2009, 20). Themistocles ruled that it was the Persian navy which was its Achilles heel. So a well-trained Athenian Navy would be the only way for Xerxes to lose and his army. Despite defeating Xerxes' Persian army via the plane of Marathon on the ground, the

Persian force that Xerxes took south with him on land was so vast that the Greeks decided to try another route to defeat the Persians. The Persian navy, however, was vast. It was composed mainly of subordinate peoples who were forced from fighting, as opposed to its army that had a core of Persian fighters (Hale 2009).

A Greek trireme illustration

Themistocles managed to build the Athenian Navy using his silver tongue. The silver found at Attica was then used by him to make the Athenian Fleet's general. Plutarch states that few men wanted to be the leaders of the Athenians against Persians. This may have been due to fear of Persian revenges should Xerxes defeat Greece. The fear did not deter all candidates. Epicydes and Themistocles both were considered finalists, but Epicydes was able to displace him using his charm. Plutarch explained, "At last, as the

Mede descending upon Hellas was deliberating who should their general? So panic-stricken were them at the danger; but Epicydes was the son of Euphemides and a popular leader who had been powerful in speech but effeminate by spirit and open for bribes. So Themistocles was afraid lest things should get to utter ruin in the event that such a man became the leader.

Themistocles held the position of general so the Athenians could have a competent leader to defeat the Persian fleet. In 480 CE, the Athenians temporarily ended all ostracisms. This allowed rich and famous citizens to return to their property to defend it. Athens was later able to reap the benefits of this policy at Battle of Salamis. The formerly exiled Aristides who was the second most powerful Athenian at that battle, fought bravely alongside his fellow countrymen (Plutarch Aristides VII).

The Greeks had two final acts to complete before Xerxes, the Persian army arrived at Attica. The ancient Greeks saw the role and actions of all their gods in every event, big and small. Poseidon provided protection for the Greek mariners. Athena also protected the city she named after her. Zeus, who sat on Mount Olympus and presided over all immortals and mortals, was a very religious person. When the Greeks needed answers to important questions regarding worldly affairs and situations, they turned to oracles. Apollo's Delphi Oracle, which was located in Delphi, was the most important one in the Greek world. (Parker 2001. 320). Herodotus recorded that Athenians approached the Oracle to ask for advice on how they should respond against the Persian army.

"Why sit down, doomed ones?" Fly to the other side of the earth, leaving behind

Home and the heights you city circles like a ring.

The body and the head should not be left in their place.

Not the feet underneath, or the hands, or the parts in between.

But all is not lost for fire and the headlong gods war

The price of a Syrian Chariot is very low.

You alone are not allowed to destroy a tower.

Don't forget to give to the pitiless fire many shrines dedicated to gods.

These are the ones who, even now, sweat, and feel fear.

Black blood runs through the roofs while it is streaming.

Prophecy must bring all that is necessary. But rise.

Haste from The Sanctuary and bow to your grief." (Herodotus. The Histories. VII. 140).

The oracle's response was confusing and troubling for the Athenians. As a sign of their faith, they decided to approach him again with olive branches in both their hands (Herodotus. The Histories VII, 141). The second prophecy, though still enigmatic in its nature, proved to be the final word on the matter. Herodotus claimed that this time the oracle said:

"Not entirely can Pallas win over the heart and soul of Olympian Zeus.

Although she prays to him with many prayers;

Yet, I will say this:

All else must be taken within Cercrops' bounds

The speed of the holy mountain of Cithaeron.

Yet Zeus, the allseeing God grants Athene her prayer

It is not possible for the wooden wall to collapse. However, it can be used to help you.

your Children.

Don't be afraid to ask for help from the Asian horsemen and women.

Or you could be still, but then turn your back and flee from the enemy.

You will truly meet him one day.

Divine Salamis, you'll bring death to women's sons

When the harvest is gathered in or the corn is spread." (Herodotus. The Histories. VII. 141).

Although the second prophecy was somewhat clearer than the first, there was a new question: what was the wooden barrier? The Athenians debated the meaning of the wooden wall. While one side believed it was an indication of the Athenian fleet, another group believed it was. Herodotus, The Histories. VII, 142.

The Athenians seemed to be at an impasse with their democratic nature. Themistocles would bridge it, not by priests or oracles but by Athens' supreme commandant and orator. The Athenian commander, who had put too much money into the Athenian naval fleet, was not going to let it get away by misinterpreting a prophecy. Therefore, he did the right thing any military commander would: he translated the prophecy. Herodotus said, "There was however an Athens person who had recently become prominent - Themistocles was Neocles's child; he now declared that the professional interpreters had misunderstood an important point. If he believed that the Athenians were the victims of the disaster, it wouldn't have been said in such gentle language. If the country's inhabitants were doomed, 'Hateful Salamis' would be a more plausible phrase than divine Salamis. In fact, the truth of the matter was that the oracle didn't refer to the Athenians. It was their enemies. The 'wooden barrier' was actually a reference to ships. So he advised his fellow citizens to get ready to meet the invaders at sea." (Herodotus. The Histories. VII. 143).

Themistocles charisma, charm, and oratorical skills prevailed again when the Athenians decided on evacuating Athens and Attica. The Athenians then made their stand at the channel between Attic Peninsula and the island Salamis.

However, the Greeks were able to retreat further south to Salamis island and the Peloponnesian peninsula. Thus, while Xerxes and his Persian army were advancing south through the kingdoms in Thrace and Macedon, a number Greek city states held a conference and created the Hellenic League. Sparta took the lead role as military leader (Herodotus. The Histories. Once Athenians selected a leader and built a navy, they could now start to implement their plan.

The Persians were moving south, so the Greeks decided to meet Xerxes' forces and give their people more time for Attica to be evacuated. A contingent of 10,000 allied Greek forces was sent under the command the Spartans to blockade Tempe, Thessaly's pass. However, it was discovered that Xerxes had gotten a march on them. The Persians managed to overcome the first failure and successfully crossed the Hellespont, crossing into northern Greece just south of Tempe. The Persians could only stop Xerxes by crossing the Hellespont in 480 BCE. In order to cross into Greece the Persians would have had to travel through Thermopylae's mountain pass, which was already a strategic site that had seen plenty of battles. The Greeks could defeat Xerxes if they could keep him at Thermopylae. The allied fleet at Artemisium could also stop the Persian navy from bypassing.

Thermopylae clearly was an important battle during the Greco/Persian Wars. However a naval engagement that took part between the Persian-Athenian fleets near Artemisium had an even greater effect on the Battle of Salamis. Herodotus claims that the Persian fleet vastly outnumbered the Greeks but that it was a draw in Herodotus' account (Herodotus. The Histories. VII, 8-200). Plutarch provides additional details, including how the Greeks used Artemisium's experience to fight the Battle of Salamis. He wrote: "The battles that were fought at the time with Barbarians ships in narrows weren't decisive about the main problem, it's true, but they were of great service to Hellenes in giving experience, since they were thus trained by actual achievements in face of danger that neither multitudes and ships." (Plutarch. Themistocles. VIII).

Plutarch's passage exposes two important aspects in naval warfare that were taught to the Athenians at Artemisium. These would be used at Salamis later. First, the Athenians were unable to fight in the narrows against a Persian fleet due to their small numbers. However, this made it less important for the Persians' numerical superiority as only a handful of ships could battle in the narrows at once. In addition, the Greeks discovered that they can stand up to a numerically superior enemy. Furthermore, the victory at Salamis was made possible by the confidence that the Battle for Artemisium gave the Athenians.

Despite the Greek fleet's impressive display at Artemisium the Persian advance was slowed down temporarily. It even provoked the wrathful Xerxes. The Greek defense of Thermopylae collapsed and they fell back to their second defensive line. It stretched across the Isthmus of Corinth landward, where the Peloponnesians - mainly Spartans - built a wall. The Salamis strit was at the other end (Hale 2009. 57). The Greeks gave up all of Attica north of the line - essentially all that Attica - in exchange for Xerxes' and the Persians.

The Persian army suffered a great deal from any Greeks who were unfortunate enough to be captured north of the defensive lines. Herodotus explained, "Along the valley of Cephisus everything was spared. Drymus, Charadra and Erochus, Tethronium. Amphicaea. Neon. Pedies. Trites. Elateia. Huampolis. Parapotamii. All these places were set ablaze, even Abae where there was a temple to Apollo that was richly furnished with offerings and treasures of all sorts. It was the location of an oracle. Unfortunately, it has been destroyed and its shrine was also burned. A few Phocians got caught in the mountains, and several women were raped multiple times by so many Persians that their bodies were burned." (Herodotus. The Histories. VIII. 33).

The Persian army reached Panopes. Upon reaching Athens, it split into two sections. Xerxes led his division to Athens and the other sacked Delphi and the temple. (Herodotus. The Histories., VIII, 34-5).

Athens was abandoned by the Persians when they finally arrived. A small force was left to defend its Acropolis. After a successful siege Xerxes directed the destruction and desecration of the Acropolis, its temples, and all other Athenians. Herodotus stated, "But the Persians solved them problem: A way of accessing the Acropolis - it was prophesied that all Athenian land upon the continents of Greece should be overthrown by Persians. A spot is just in front the Acropolis. This is the place where the ascent is so steep no guard was put up because it was thought impossible that any man could climb it. Here, near Cercrops daughter Aglaurus' shrine, some soldiers managed the steep climb up the cliff. . . They took the treasures from the temple and set fire to everything on the Acropolis, leaving behind none of them. Xerxes, now absolute ruler of Athens dispatched a rider with news for

Artabanus to Susa." (Herodotus. The Histories. VIII. 53-54).

It was on water that the crucial battle would occur, not on land. The Battle of Salamis, which was much like the Battle of Artemisium, was fought through a narrow channel. This channel separates the Attic Peninsula from the island of Salamis. The island is known by the name Salamis, but it is not clear whether the name refers to an island or to a town in ancient sources (Hammond 1956, 37).

Pausanias, the 1st century CE Greek geograph, was the first to write about the history and physical description for Salamis. His writings included the following: "Salamis is over Eleusis. It stretches as far away as the territory in Megara. Cychreus is the one who gave the island this name. He called it Salamis after his mother Salamis (the daughter of Asopus). The Aeginetans colonized it with

Telamon. Philaeus the son Eurysaces, a son of Ajax is believed to have given the island over to Athenians. After discovering their treachery, the Athenians expelled all the Salaminians from the island many years later." (Pausanias Description Of Greece, I, 35.1-2).

Although the Battle of Salamis took place at sea, historical records cannot provide an exact picture of their position. However, there are two other landmarks that can be seen on land from the Battle of Salamis. Xerxes viewed all of the battle from a throne below Mount Aegaleos. Therefore, modern scholars have his exact location placed opposite the island Salamis, and above the Heracleum Temple, which was in the narrowest part (Hammond 56, 38). The location of the Battle of Salamis' limited land fighting was on the island of Pystalia (Morkot 1997,

76), just before Salamis (Hammond 1956 38).

The most remarkable aspect of the physical layout for the channel of Salamis is the ability to fit so many triremes into such a small area. The accounts of Herodotus & Plutarch along with Aeschylus' drama The Persians, can provide an insight into the size of both fleets. Plutarch mentions Aeschylus to be the source of the Persian fleet's size in his account (Plutarch. Themistocles.XIV.1), but he only provides the number of Attic (Athenian), ships in his account (Plutarch. Themistocles.XIV.1). Herodotus agrees with his account, as he writes that the Athenians numbered 183 triremes (and accounted for half) of the Greek fleet. Aeschylus mentioned the numbers of both the fleets in the passage. This scene was where a Persian messenger relayed the story of the defeat to Atossa, Xerxes' mom. The scene reads, "If number ships might win the fight. Believe me, queen. Our victory had been ours. The Greeks could only tell thirty ships ten times, and ten of the best equipment. Xerxes numbered a 1000 ships, two hundred sail, and seven of rapid wing alongside." (Aeschylus, 312). N.G.L., a modern historian, was able to draw a conclusion based on the ancient accounts. Hammond placed the Persian total vessels at 1,407, while the Greeks at 3,807. This figure includes some Greek defectors from Persian ships who arrived in Greece to join their nationmen after the Battle of Artemisium. Hammond 1956, 40.

Despite the differences in numbers many major battles are won before the battle has even begun. The Battle of Salamis was no other example of this. The key aspect of any military strategy is to decide where and when it will be fought. Commanders who are able to choose the time and place to engage their enemy have two advantages. The Persian fleet advanced towards Salamis while the Persian army was nearing the Isthmus of Corinth. But not all of Greece, particularly the Spartans, were convinced Salamis was the right location. The wise commander of the Athenian, Themistocles understood that victory for the Greeks would depend on holding the channel in Salamis. To convince his countrymen, he used his oratory skills once again. Herodotus said that Themistocles had a plan. He stated, "Now for my Plan: it will bring if you accept it: First, I believe we will be fighting with narrow waters. And there, with our inferior number, we will win. Provided things go as we reasonably expect. Fight in a restricted space is better for us than the open sea. Salamis, where our women and children have been placed, will be preserved. Thirdly, you'll be fighting for the defense of the Peloponnese in this area just as much if you withdraw to the Isthmus. You won't draw the Persian army into the Peloponnese, unless you have the courage to follow my advice. I think they will defeat us at sea if they do. If they do, they won't advance to attack you on Attica or come any further. They will retreat in disorder. Megara Aegina and Salamis will be preserved - where an ancient oracle foretold that we would win.

Themistocles has deep knowledge of the Greek psyche and intelligence. Themistocles understood his fleet's capabilities after the Battle of Artemisium. He also knew how to win at Salamis. Fighting in narrow channels benefited the numerically superior Greek fleet because it prevented the Persian fleet navigating a diekplous or surrounding it. Athenian general appealed also to the Greeks' emotions by pointing out that they would not be stopped until they were defeated by the Persians and that Delphi's oracle foretold that their wooden wall (of ship) would be victorious.

The Spartans as well as other Peloponnesians appeared to have been appeased with Themistocles speech. However, Themistocles was a wily Athenian commander who had one last maneuver that would make it possible for the Greeks to win at Salamis. Themistocles realized the Greek army could not retreat from Themistocles' command and would continue to fight fiercely. Themistocles feared that many of the Peloponnesians would abandon their homes in order to return to Greece. So, he devised a strategy that combined deception with guile. Herodotus explains, "At this point Themistocles was afraid he'd be outvoted. So he quietly left the meeting and sent a man to the Persian fleet in a boat with instructions about what to say. The man - Sicinnus -- was one Themistocles' slaves. He used this time to tend to his sons. . . Sicinnus, following his instructions, made his way towards the Persian commanders. He stated: 'I am carrying a secret message from the Athenian commander. This communication is well-wisher to you king and hopes to win the Persian war. He informed me that the Greeks have plans to flee and are afraid. Stop them from slipping through you fingers and you have the opportunity to be a great success. They will fight each other with daggers, and you will witness the pro-Persians among them fighting the rest.

Themistocles could not see if his plan was working under darkness. Aristides (another Athenian) sailed peacefully through the Persian fleet, leaving behind the allied Greek state Aegina. Aristides offered his help to Themistocles in spite of the conflict between the esteemed Athenians. Plutarch stated that "O Themistocles", he said, "If it is wise, we will at last lay aside vain contention, and start a salutary & honourable rivalry, in emulous battles to save Hellas. thou as commanding General, I as assistant Counsellor, since I at the outset learn that the only one who adopted the best strategy, urging as many as thous to face a decisive war here in narrows as may soonest to get to win, and to win the narrows as soon possible."

A statue depicting Aristides

This was actually a crucial moment for the Greeks, before the battle started. Aristides, who would prove indispensable in the landing battle, joined Themistocles' fleet and saw Themistocles' trick. Herodotus told us that Themistocles had not only succeeded in his plan, since the Persian fleet circled the Greeks, but that he was so sure of himself that he didn't mind how the Greeks would react if he revealed that he was behind the attack. However, you can give them the good information yourself. If I tell them that they invented it, they will doubt me. You can then go in and complete the report. If they believe that you, good. But, if they don't, they can still make the report. For if we are surrounded like you claim, escape is impossible.

Themistocles ploy was effective because it forced the Greeks into fighting to the last ship. He also displayed his skills as a commander by selecting the beginning of battle. The ancient sources agree with this assertion that the Battle of Salamis occurred at a time when it was most important. Plutarch states that Themistocles selected a time that was favorable to the sleek, low to water Greek triremes. Inasmuch, Themistocles did not send his triremes to battle against the Barbarian ships until the hour of dawn, which brought fresh air from the sea and a breeze through the Strait. The Hellenic ships did not suffer from this breeze as they were low in water and small. But for the Barbarian vessels, with their large sterns and high decks and slow movements when getting under way it was fatal.

At dawn, just before combat began the leaders of both armies took up their places. Xerxes sat in relative safety at the shore, allowing him to observe the battle. Plutarch states that Xerxes sat at the break of dawn on a high platform, overlooking his armament. This place was, Phanodemus said, "above the Heracleium," where only one narrow passage separates Attica Island from Attica." (Plutarch. Themistocles., XIII).

Xerxes remained seated on his perch during the entire battle, never in harm. This contrasted sharply with Themistocles. He took Themistocles' place on a trireme amongst his soldiers and roused them with his oratorical skills. Herodotus does not have a complete version of the speech (Zali 2013, 467) and it is paraphrased. Themistocles used standard Greek rhetorical skills (Zali 2013. 462) to exhort the men to defend their superior nature against their enemies. It is easy to see how the speech fits into the larger picture of Greek victory in the Battle of Salamis. Themistocles, an expert at rhetoric and strategy, used his full skills to exhort Greeks to fight fearlessly and against overwhelming odds. The speech, though it may not have been decisive for the Greek victory in the Battle of Salamis was still part of the "wooden wall" prophesied by the oracle.

One of the most intriguing aspects of Battle of Salamis, at the very least in terms of military maneuvers is that no ancient sources mention a diekplous (Wallinga 1990 148). Some historians now believe that the Phoenician boats at the rear ranks the Persian fleet were meant to prevent a Greek dasplous (Hale 2009, 64). But it's impossible to be certain because of the silence in the ancient sources.

The Greek fleet was organized in a single line, against the Salamis shore. Although the word diekplous is not used to describe maneuvers on Salamis, a close look at the sources reveals it was on Themistocles' mind. It is clear that the Athenian commander chose Salamis' narrow channel, which was similar to Artemisium in topography, to stop a Persian siekplous. It is possible that one was prevented by the Greeks, as the ancient sources do not describe it in their accounts. But, either way, the narrows stopped the Persian fleet from performing the maneuver. The Greeks, for their part did not have the numbers necessary to perform one.

Map showing the positions and coordinates of both navies

The Persian fleet encountered a thin Greek line made up of ships from Aegina (right wing), Spartan ships in middle and the Athenian fleet (left wing) against the Phoenicians. As the Persian fleet advanced towards the Greeks, war cries and trumpets erupted out of the Greek line. Aeschylus writes, "Then a fierce trumpet's vocal blazed overhead; and on salt sea flood forthwith with the oars, measured plash and descended, all their lines, with dexterous speeds displayed, stood alongside the opposing front. The right wing came first, then all the fleet went down, and there was a loud shout. 'SONS OF GREEKS! ADVANCE! Your country is free, your children are free, and your wives are free! THE ALTARS OPTIONS OF YOUR NATIVE GODS DELIVER, AND YOUR AGENCY TOMBS ARE NOW AT STAKE!" (Aeschylus and The Persians, 313)

The Persians, possibly overanxious and aggressive due their numerical superiority moved toward the Greek line. But the line held and even the back rowed in retreat in order face the Persian ships with its rams. The Persian fleet, despite its size, was still at a disadvantage as their broadsides became exposed to the Greek deadly rams (Hale 2009: 47). Plutarch also wrote about this first engagement, although their details differ slightly. Herodotus said, "The entire fleet now got underway, and in no time the Persians was on them. The Greeks checked the way and started to return astern. But they were close to running aground, when Ameinias (commander of an Athenian boat) drove ahead and rammed an opponent vessel. The Greek fleet was able to see the two ships in distress and joined together. Ameinias and the rest of them rushed to Ameinias for help and the action began. (Herodotus' The Histories VIII, 84).

Plutarch does not mention Ameinias but his account of early fighting at Battle of Salamis doesn't include that. It is however more informative in terms strategy and maneuvers. Plutarch pointed out that Lycomedes (an Athenian captain) was the first person to capture an enemy vessel. He then dedicated it to Apollo, Phlya's Laurel bearer. The rest put on an equality in number with their foes. The Barbarians had to attack them in detachments in narrow straits and so they ran afoul, routed the others, though they resisted them till the evening drew.

Plutarch's account, while shorter (in fact, his complete account of fighting is just this passage), is more comprehensive and reveals more about the successful strategies employed in the battle by the Greeks. This battle was a pivotal one because of the narrow channel that separated Attica from Salamis. It proved to be a deterrent to the Persians' numerical superiority. The channel's bottleneck allowed the Greeks to fight the Persians in a limited manner, as they only had to do so one at a moment. This prevented the Persians from performing the diekplous maneuver.

After the initial fighting, the battle moved quickly into the second, crucial phase. It was either frustration at the inability to encircle and destroy the Greek fleet, poor commanders or a combination of both. The Persian fleet quickly displayed its lackluster discipline and cut its line (Hale 2009, 69). The Battle of Salamis was decided after the Persian line had broken.

It was the battle in which the Persian fleet lost to the Greeks. The Persian line was broken and each ship was left on its own, but the Greeks stood firm and decided to fight their respective battles. Herodotus explained that the Persian fleet was severely damaged in battle with the Aeginetans (the Athenians) accounting for many of their ships. The Greek fleet worked as a whole and while the Persians lost formation and weren't fighting on any plan, this was what was going to happen." (Herodotus in The Histories, VIII: 86).

The Greeks beat the Persians in ship to ship combat. They used their rams to sink their enemies' ships. The Persians performed well in most instances when they used the method to board and then fight on the desk of ship (Hammond 1956; 48). But such cases were rare at Salamis.

www.ingramcontent.com/pod-product-compliance
Lightning Source LLC
Chambersburg PA
CBHW071338120626
46546CB00002B/611